D0787489

WITHDRAWN

Damaged, Obsolete, or Surplus

Jackson County Library Services

Deschutes

Other Books by Dave Hughes

The Complete Book of Western Hatches (with Rick Hafele)
An Angler's Astoria
American Fly Tying Manual
Western Fly Fishing Guide
Handbook of Hatches
Western Streamside Guide
Reading the Water
Tackle and Technique for Taking Trout

Copyright 1990 • Dave Hughes
Front Cover Photo: Bill McMillan
Back Cover Photo: Frank Amato
Book Design: Joyce Herbst
Map by: Esther Paleo
ISBN 0-936608-91-9 Softbound
ISBN 0-936608-92-7 Hardbound

Frank Amato Publications
P.O. Box 82112 • Portland, Oregon 97282
(503) 653-8108 FAX: 653-2766
Printed in Hong Kong

DESCHUTES

Dave Hughes

Frank Amato Publications

JACKSON COUNTY LIBRARY SERVICES
MEDFORD, OREGON 97501

About the author: Dave Hughes is a professional outdoor writer and amateur aquatic entomologist. His affection for the Deschutes River is rooted in his youth, spent in the dampness of the Oregon coast. He loves nothing better than to roam the expansive dry country, alongside the big river, fly rod in one hand and crushed leaves of the strong-scented sage in the other. He was taught by his father that the smell of sagebrush clears the head and cures a cold. Hughes has been crossing the mountains to take that cure along the river for 20 years now.

Articles by Hughes have appeared in *Flyfishing, Salmon Trout Steelheader, Fly Fisherman, The Fly Fisher, Rod & Reel, Outdoor Life, and Field & Stream.* He has long been a popular lecturer at sportsmen's shows, fly fishing conclaves, and club meetings or banquets. He is a charter member of the Rainland Fly Casters, was founding president of Oregon Trout in 1983, and received the Lew Jewett Memorial Life Membership award from the Federation of Fly Fishers in 1985.

Below: *Take-out at the mouth of the Deschutes.*
JIM SCHOLLMEYER

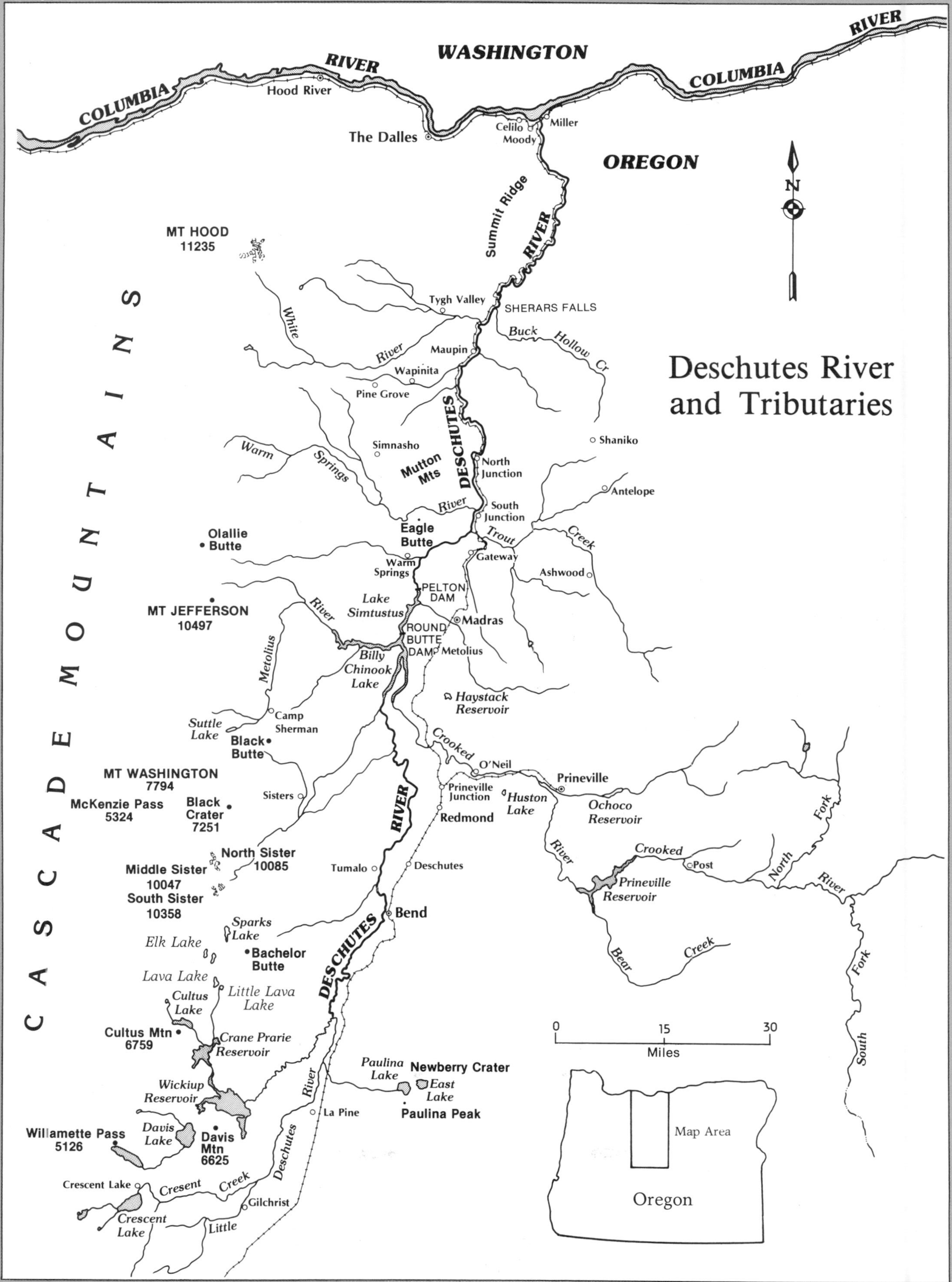

Deschutes River and Tributaries

WASHINGTON

OREGON

COLUMBIA RIVER

COLUMBIA RIVER

Hood River

The Dalles

Celilo
Moody
Miller

Summit Ridge

Buck Hollow Cr

SHERARS FALLS

DESCHUTES RIVER

Shaniko

Antelope

Creek

Ashwood

Tygh Valley
Maupin
Wapinita
Pine Grove

Simnasho

Mutton Mts

North Junction
South Junction
Trout
Gateway
Creek

River

Madras
Metolius

DESCHUTES

Eagle Butte

Warm Springs

PELTON DAM
ROUND BUTTE DAM

Lake Simtustus

Billy Chinook Lake

Haystack Reservoir

O'Neil

Prineville Junction
Redmond

Crooked

Crooked River

Ochoco Reservoir

Prineville

Prineville Reservoir

Post

North Fork

South Fork

River

Bear

Creek

Deschutes

White River

Warm Springs River

River

Metolius

Camp Sherman

Suttle Lake

Olallie Butte

MT JEFFERSON 10497

Black Butte

Sisters

MT WASHINGTON 7794
McKenzie Pass 5324

Black Crater 7251

North Sister 10085
Middle Sister 10047
South Sister 10358

Sparks Lake

Bachelor Butte

Little Lava Lake

Elk Lake

Lava Lake

Cultus Lake

Cultus Mtn 6759

Crane Prarie Reservoir

Wickiup Reservoir

Davis Lake

Davis Mtn 6625

Willamette Pass 5126

Crescent Lake

Crescent Lake

Crescent Creek

Little

Gilchrist

Deschutes River

La Pine

DESCHUTES RIVER

Bend

Tumalo

Deschutes

Paulina Lake
East Lake
Newberry Crater
Paulina Peak

Huston Lake

MT HOOD 11235

CASCADE MOUNTAINS

N

Oregon
Map Area

Miles
0 15 30

Introduction

The Deschutes River has a meaning to me that has not always been clear. But now I think I understand it, after 20 years of fishing there.

One of my favorite places on the river is the long curve of grassy bank just upstream from the Deschutes Club gate, a few miles above Maupin. I go there not because the fishing is good, but because the napping is good.

I first stopped there one day in the summer of the year I had back surgery. I did not yet know if I could fish again as I had before. I was still afraid of rivers. I parked my car at the locked gate, got out, and saw that sweep of green grass creeping to the edge of the river in the hot sun. A scattering of alders sprinkled some shade on the grass. It looked like an excellent place for a snooze. I pulled on my waders, gathered together the various pieces of stuff that can add up to a fly fishing outfit if one wants them to, and walked down through the sagebrush to the river.

Facing page: *The Deschutes begins as a small headwater stream in the jackpine country southwest of Bend, just off the Cascade Lakes Highway. Its water seeps off the east slopes of the Cascade Mountains, is filtered through a lava aquifer, and eventually gathers to become the official source of the river at Little Lava Lake.* LOREN IRVING

I sat in the shade of an alder next to the water, and looked out over a broad and shallow flat. It was sunstruck; all of the rounded cobble on its bottom shone visibly and clear. I saw no fish, so I lay back and went to sleep.

I woke up, I don't know how long later, because the shade of the tree had gone away from me, had left me lying in the scorching sun, had migrated out to cast a mottled semicircle of darkness over the water at the edge of the flat. I sat up, examined the flat for fish again, still saw none, so I stood up and got ready to go. Then my mind, not my eye, sorted out from their dappled surroundings a small pod of trout feeding in the same shade I had earlier enjoyed. They were only a few feet from shore.

They nosed among the bottom stones, tilted down, feeding in water only a foot deep. Their upraised tails sent slight swirls to the surface whenever they dislodged some bit of food and shot eagerly after it. There were six of them, all larger than 12 inches, which made them all big ones in my eyes, in those days. They were close to me where they worked just out from the bank, not more than 20 feet from where I had snoozed.

It was obvious that the trout dislodged and chased down to death various aquatic insect nymphs and larvae and other organisms. But I felt they could be tempted upward to a dry fly because the water was so shallow. They wouldn't have far to go to get one.

I sneaked out of there through the sage, walked downstream, assembled my tackle so it made some sense, and waded in below the fish. I crept out to where I could cover them by casting upstream and in toward the bank. I dropped a dry caddis pattern lightly above the fish. It floated primly down over the pod. Nothing disturbed it. When it had drifted downstream below them, I lifted the fly quietly, cast it again, fished out its drift, then cast it again. And again and again. Nothing happened.

Above: *The broad sweeping bends of the Deschutes, and its shallow flats, are richest, and offer the best fishing. Sunlight strikes down through the water, causes plant growth, and plants feed aquatic insects, which in their turn feed trout.* SCOTT RIPLEY

Below: *The desert bursts with flowers in spring, but many of them are small or hidden among sages and grasses. You've got to take time to look for them, and then add time to appreciate them.* RENA LANGILLE

I tried other dry flies. Lots of them. Nothing ever happened. So I gave up on dries and crept up farther onto the flat, so I could cast straight in toward the trout. I tied on a tiny nymph, probably a muskrat-bodied Gray Nymph because that was my favorite in those days, and I always tried it first. From then on the trout were easy. I hooked one on the first cast, let it run downstream out of the pod, then tightened up on it, played it tired, landed and quickly released it. When I let it go, it dug in furiously with its tail, arrowed out over the sunlit flat, and disappeared into the darkness of the deep and untouchable water beyond it.

The rest of the trout were unaware of this event. They went on feeding. I cast the nymph again, hooked another trout, drew it away from the pod as I had the first, and landed it. It was a native redside rainbow, in dark spawning colors, red on its sides, 17 inches long. I released it, too, and it shot across the flat to the safety of deep water.

It took several casts to hook another trout. It bolted through the scant remains of the pod and sent them galloping across the flat, toward the depth and darkness that nobody could ever reach to fish. I brought this last trout to my hand and killed it, waded to shore and cleaned it. I sliced open its viscera to see what it had eaten. It contained three large, black salmonfly nymphs, a few smaller cased caddis larvae, and a salt and peppering of dark-eyed alevins with whitish, almost transparent bodies. These were probably summer steelhead, chinook salmon, or even cannibalized redside trout, their futures ruined.

I walked up from the river through the gray sage with the one trout for my dinner. But I also carried with me a small refreshment from the nap, and a certain renewal from having fished the Deschutes, even a shallow and easily-waded portion of it, for the first time after having had back surgery.

* * *

A year later I drove from my home in Astoria, over the Cascades, to fish the Deschutes again. It was a three-day weekend after a long wet winter that had trailed too far into what should have been spring. Finally the sun broke through. I wanted to smell sage for the first time, to see and feel and hear the river, to coax some of the winter stiffness out of my bones, out of my brain.

The first day of the three-day weekend I fished upstream from Maupin, rock-hopping along the steep, brushy banks, casting a caddis dry into likely-looking places behind boulders and under sweeps of bunchgrass and willow. Trout after trout rose up to take the fly. That first day I caught so many fish that I felt another day of it would be either an excess, or a let-down. On the second day I left the river and drove up to Timberline Lodge on Mt. Hood, had a hot chocolate, then drove down through the Hood River Valley to enjoy the flaming of orchard blossoms that ignites the valley once a year.

On the third day of the three-day weekend I mowed my lawn at home, whistling as I pushed the mower through the damp Astoria grass.

Sometimes one day of renewal is enough.

* * *

I have had some very successful fishing trips to the Deschutes, trips where I caught lots of fish, including an occasional trout that I judged to be a big one by the standards I set for them. I could tell of those trips here, but it seems not to need doing, because successful fishing is not what I go to the Deschutes River to get.

Fishing from boats is not allowed on the Deschutes. The river is so wide and deep and powerful in most places that only a particle of it, along the edges, can be walked on or waded in and fished well. The rest of it is left untouched, unfished. It is left to grow trout, to renew the portion of the river that is slowly depleted by fishermen.

It is a clumsy comparison, but I think I understand now that my reasons for going to the Deschutes are related to those wide expanses of river that can never be fished. I go to the river to fish a little, when I need fishing, to nap along the banks, when I need sleep, to be with my friends again, when I need to renew friendships. And I go there just to gaze out over those great expanses of swift-flowing water that cannot be used.

The river reminds me that there are expanses of myself that cannot be used, expanses that replenish the shoreline of me, the part that is walked on and waded in when I work, when I perform the daily doings that propel me along the path of life. The Deschutes, the rich river that renews itself, has become my own river of renewal.

If you use it right, the Deschutes can become your river of renewal, too.

DLH
Astoria, OR
March, 1989

Above: *Sage banks and alder-covered islands define the river in its more placid reaches, which are few but beautiful.* BRIAN O'KEEFE

Dedication

Once while wading a riffle near Maupin, I stopped fishing to watch a freight train hurry past on the bank above me. I waved at the engineer as I always do and he tooted back as they sometimes do. Halfway down the train an empty low-sided car clattered along, a man standing still in it in serene contrast to all of the bustle and rushing wind of the train. He leaned against the side of the car and gazed out over the river, looking lofty for all the elevation the tracks above the river and then the car above the tracks gave him. I waved at him, too.

He raised his right arm and hand straight out toward me and lowered his head slightly at the same time, and it gave the instant impression of a high priest giving a blessing.

This book is dedicated to him: to that bum giving blessings to fishermen along the river, whoever he might be, wherever his path might have taken him.

Above: *Wild rose is a common shrub along the river, and blooms brightly in summer.*
RENA LANGILLE

Right: *The Deschutes is one of the West's largest and most powerful rivers. You never fail to feel small alongside it.* DAMIAN DLUGOLECKI

Facing page: *Many miles of the Deschutes can be reached only by boat, or by a very ambitious hiker. When you get into those reaches, you are likely to have some river to yourself. This water is at the lower end of famous Whitehorse Rapids.* L.A. ROSER

Contents

Land Forms-Animal Forms

Sixty million years ago, long before it was declared a state, not much of Oregon held its nose above water. The waves of a warm sea lapped against highlands where the Blue Mountains stand now, in the northeast corner, and other highlands in the southwest corner. That was all.

Then a gigantic plate beneath the Pacific Ocean got restless — it still is — and nudged its way under the west edge of the North American continental plate, hoisting it slowly upward. When the level floor of what had once been the sea arose, it formed a plain in what is now central and eastern Oregon. The elevation of this plain was only slightly above that of the waters that slowly receded from its westward edge. Rocks of those first lands to arise in the central plain still hold fossil shells of mollusks and other forms of life in seawater.

Records of the time tell us that the land was swampy, and was drained by lazy, meandering streams depositing deltas of silt, sand, and mud along a shore which wasn't where it is now. There were no Cascade Mountains. The streams, heavy with tropical rains, came out of the east and entered the ocean in the area that is now the Willamette Valley. When ancestors to the Cascades began to seethe up, still tens of millions of years ago, they were west of where they are now, perched at the edge of where the ocean was then. These mountains were violently volcanic, but they were not high enough to keep those westering rivers from wending ways around them.

Mammals migrated to Oregon, possibly as the land rose, browsing west across the flat, swampy plain. The Clarno area, not many miles east of today's Deschutes River, yields the first signs of land life in Oregon, in the Eocene epoch, beginning about 55 million years ago. The area was semi-tropical then. Its fossil record includes rhinos, tiny horses with four toes, and tapirs. Plants were palms, figs, pecans, and walnuts, though they were not planted in rows just then. Crocodiles lurked along the rivers and swam the shallow shores of lakes.

Mammalian evidence is missing for ten million years or so after the deposits in the Clarno beds, which doesn't mean the animals were absent, just that they failed to leave their bones in deposits where man could find them. When mammals showed up again in the John Day fossil beds, starting in the Oligocene epoch, 35 million years ago, they also left their ancient remains along the Crooked River and in what is now the Deschutes River Canyon.

These John Day fossils were different characters from the earlier animals found at Clarno. Included were deer with club-like horns, camels, and saber-toothed cats. Giant pigs were apparently unfortunate in having giant dogs to hound after them. The presence of three-toed horses indicates the discarding of digits on the evolutionary path toward the single-toed horses we ride today. Plants were dominated by maple, sycamore, and ginkgo forests.

Intermittent Columbia River Basalt lava flows spread over the land for millions of years starting in the Miocene epoch, 25 million years ago. Tier on tier of these dark flows are exposed along the Deschutes River today; they are the prime feature you see as you hike or drift the lower 100 miles of river, lifting your eyes to the canyon walls.

Above: *Yellowhead blackbirds depend on marshy ground for nesting sites. Their populations are not great along the arid Deschutes, but sighting a male keeping a watchful eye on its territory is far from uncommon.* MARGARET THOMPSON MATHEWSON

Facing page: *The broad, shallow lakes and reservoirs in the scenic Deschutes River headwaters region are rich in aquatic insect life, which fuels trout and makes them grow to sizes that are weighed in pounds, not measured in inches.* LOREN IRVING

These black basalts were extruded through large cracks in the earth's crust, in what was then the flat plain east of what is now the course of the Deschutes river. They were fluid flows rather than violent eruptions, oozing out and over the land rather than blasting up and raining down on it. The largest flows covered areas up to 10,000 square miles, which makes a square 100 miles on the side, which is a lot of Oregon to bury at once under molten lava. The flows altered the face of what had been the flat central and eastern Oregon plain.

This plain was further wrenched by the uplifting of the interior plateau, the upheaval of the Ochoco Mountains, and the slow rising and sudden snapping off, rising and snapping — can you still feel echoed rumblings from those ancient earthquakes? — of what became the fault-block systems of Steens Mountain and the abrupt Warner and Abert rims.

Above: *The Columbia basalt flows in the lower Deschutes canyon extruded over the earth layer upon layer during a period that lasted millions of years. The river, when turned north by the rising Cascade Mountains three to four million years ago, began cutting down through them in the same fashion: layer by patient layer. Each of those black bands high in the hills once formed the bed of the river.* FRANK AMATO

Right: *View from inside a cave above the river. It is hard to stand inside a cave like this one, and look out at the view, without wondering what life was like for all of our ancestors when what they saw from the mouth of a cave comprised their world.* JIM SCHOLLMEYER

Facing page: *Indian carvings and lava castellations above the river.* SCOTT RIPLEY

Early artistic drawings speculating on these prehistoric days tend to show strange animals in a land of tropical palms and violent volcanoes, the dumb beasts watching over their shoulders with furrowed brows as mountain tops blow smoke and spit fire. The drawings had most of it right: the animals of the day were strange, the plants were palm-like, and those seething scenes did happen, minus the beastly furrowed brows.

More often, in the land that was to become central Oregon, great lava flows absorbed everything in their way, leaving a few highlands as scorched islands in black-rock seas when things finally cooled. Animals migrated back into the areas only after erosion had time to form soil, and vegetation had time to take root in it. This took hundreds to thousands of years after each flow.

The ancestral Cascades, in a north-south line just east of what is now the Willamette Valley, were not high enough to form much of a block to Pacific storms until relatively recent times. Rivers ran heavy with warm rains. When lava flows blocked their courses, they formed vast inland lakes in the landscape of the interior basin, east of the current Deschutes.

On the western side of the current course of the Deschutes, two generations of volcanic mountains shaped the land. The first were those active ancestors to the present High Cascades. These older and lower mountains rose and smoldered in the long period that began 60 million years ago, when the giant geologic plates began to butt against each other. The mountains were smaller than those that make up the Cascade Range now, but

they caused countless detonations more powerful than the one at St. Helens in 1981.

About 5 million years ago these early Cascades apparently subsided into the earth's crust under their own weight. Remnants of them show today in pinnacled peaks such as Three Fingered Jack and Broken Top. Rocks still exposed in the gorges of the upper Deschutes, Crooked, and Metolius rivers reveal to geologists part of the story of those ancestral mountains. The second generation of volcanoes are the Cascade Mountains that we know today: Hood, Jefferson, and South Sister, among others. Their formation began 4-1/2 million years ago. As St. Helens loudly announced, it goes on to this day.

The arising of the High Cascades caused several changes in the Deschutes River region. They spilled lava all around, and sent repeated finger flows out into the area that is now the upper Deschutes. They shot ash into the air, causing heavy deposits to filter down over the lakes and plains east of the mountains. The land that now contains Madras, Redmond and Bend was struck by what in geologic retrospect appears to be constant calamity, though there must have been long periods of peacefulness in between.

The new mountains, unlike their predecessors, were high enough to be a buttress against Pacific storms, and to cause a rain shadow on the eastern side. Rainfall was reduced to an estimated 40 inches per year, more than the 10 inches that falls there now, but far less than the tropical wetness that had fallen for all the previous millions of years. As the climate changed, the interior gradually became cooler. Plant life shifted from tropical trees, ferns, and giant horsetails to grasslands and deciduous forests.

The prehistoric Deschutes Basin was a relatively flat area, interrupted by lava flows and large lakes, but without the deep river canyons we know today. Animals feeding on the plain and around the lake margins, during the most recent million years of the intermittent Ice Ages, included giant beavers, camels, horses, rhinos, and mastodons. There is evidence — stouten your leader tippet — of salmonids that were up to 8 feet long.

The formation of the High Cascades, in the epoch beginning 4-1/2 million years ago, blocked the west-flowing Deschutes, and turned it northward toward the Columbia.

Left: This is slack water of the middle Deschutes, where it has been tamed by dams and irrigation diversions. Though it does hold a few big browns, the entire reach is not anything like the wild river it once was. Note the sharply eroded hillsides; these are relatively recent Newberry Crater lava flows, and the river has had only a thousand years or so to cut its way through them. SCOTT RIPLEY

The upper river and its headwater tributaries began eroding a course through hundreds of feet of lava deposited by the violent formation of both the low ancestral Cascades and the present High Cascades. The lower 100 miles of river were forced to cut northward across the broad virgin expanses of the Columbia River basalt flows. That is why the lower river is considered youthful by geologists. It has sharp canyon walls and no significant floodplain. In geological terms, it has only been working at its course for a short while, 3 to 4 million years.

Part of the upper river, which is loosely defined as that half of the river above the power dams, just upstream from the town of Warm Springs, was given a final shaping by later events, and is even younger.

Above: *Steelhead are detonations. They leave for the sea as tiny smolts, then return with every inch turned into a pound, and with the strength of the ocean to fuel their fights. They make dashing runs, bold leaps, and always manage to take most of the fight well into your backing line. The outcome is never certain until the fish is finally held in your hands. Sometimes you've got to fight the pushy river at the same time, your feet probing for secure footing while the fish dances around at the edge of control.* ANDY ANDERSON

Below: *Some of the flowers that can be found along the river arrived as domestics. Others are wild. The author once took a morning walk through the spring hills and came across more than twenty-five varieties, fewer than half of which, like these, would be found in the wildflower books on the region.* RENA LANGILLE

We've all heard the story of Mt. Mazama, the great mountain that blew up and scattered its top across a wide region, leaving the hole that became Crater Lake. It's a strange story, and it happened less than 7,000 years ago. Its affects were felt throughout the West, much more massively than the St. Helens eruption. The upper Deschutes Basin lies within about 50 miles of Mazama. A layer of ash fell on it, burying artifacts that prove Indians were already living there. But another event had more influence on the shape of the upper river. It ended just yesterday, in one way of thinking about it.

Mt. Newberry rose to be the highest peak in the Paulina Mountains, 20 to 30 miles directly to the east of the headwaters of the Deschutes, the part of the river upstream from the current site of Bend. Newberry erupted a little more than 1,000 years ago; its crater to-day contains East and Paulina lakes. The eruption was followed by lava outpourings from ruptures in the sides of the slopes. Molton lava ran into watercourses, filled them, and ran downstream to find its way west to the Deschutes. It filled the river canyon and turned to rush downstream. More lava from Newberry vented northward, filled the canyon of the Crooked River, the largest eastern tributary of the Deschutes, and followed that canyon until it met the other flows moving down the main Deschutes River bed. The combined river of lava did not cool and stop until it reached almost to the site of Warm Springs.

The Deschutes River was forced to cut a new channel through these flows from the Newberry volcano. The present channel of the river, in the reach from above Bend downstream to Culver and the lakes behind the power dams, is fresh, still eroding its way into the new rock, plunging down steeply and leaping over waterfalls where it hasn't had time to find a gentler way to cross hard lava flows. The canyon from Bend to Redmond and beyond is cut almost abruptly into the land; its walls are steep, and tumbled with black rock sloughed off the cliffed canyon sides.

Lava from Newberry also shaped miles of the river upstream from Bend. It formed a blockage at the current site of Benham Falls, and dammed the river for centuries. The resulting natural impoundment deposited fine soil and silt across a broad area. When the block was broken, creating the falls, it left flatlands and meadows in the upstream area where man-made Wickiup and Crane Prairie reservoirs now deposit their own fine soil and silt.

The two separate and dissimilar geographies of the upper and lower Deschutes are the result of their separate geologic histories. The upper river, with the exception of its placid reaches above the blockage at Benham Falls, has had almost no time at all to cut a canyon into or around recent lava flows that filled the old channel. As a result, it is a rougher and more tumbled river, with a course that is steeper, in a sharper and shallower canyon than that of the lower river. Anybody who has ever waded or walked it can attest that sections of the upper river have a lot of jagged edges left.

The lower river has had a few million years, a short time speaking in geological terms, but a lot longer than the upper river, to erode a course through the successive tiers of Columbia River basalts. Its canyon is deep, and still steep, but not as brutally sharp as the canyon of the upper river. There has not been enough time to erode a broad riverbottom, or to work out the peaceful riffle to run to pool structure of a more mature river. The lower Deschutes has the beginnings of that structure in its sweeping bends, giant riffles, and broad gravel bars. But the most common water type is the long, deep run, where you would never dare wade and fish. It is this youthful geology of the river, combined with the regulation against fishing from a boat, that puts so much water out of reach, and makes it a river of renewal.

The succession of lower river rapids that cause rafters to whoop are caused by underlying basalts through which the river is still cutting. The hydraulics that toss boats around are the river's patient drills, grinding away at another of the great lava floods that once flattened and denuded the land.

Right: *These towering palisades, above the lower Crooked River, were formed when the only major west-flowing tributary to the Deschutes was blocked by lava flows that snaked right down its ancient channel, and the river was forced to cut a new one.*
MARTY SHERMAN

Transitional Man

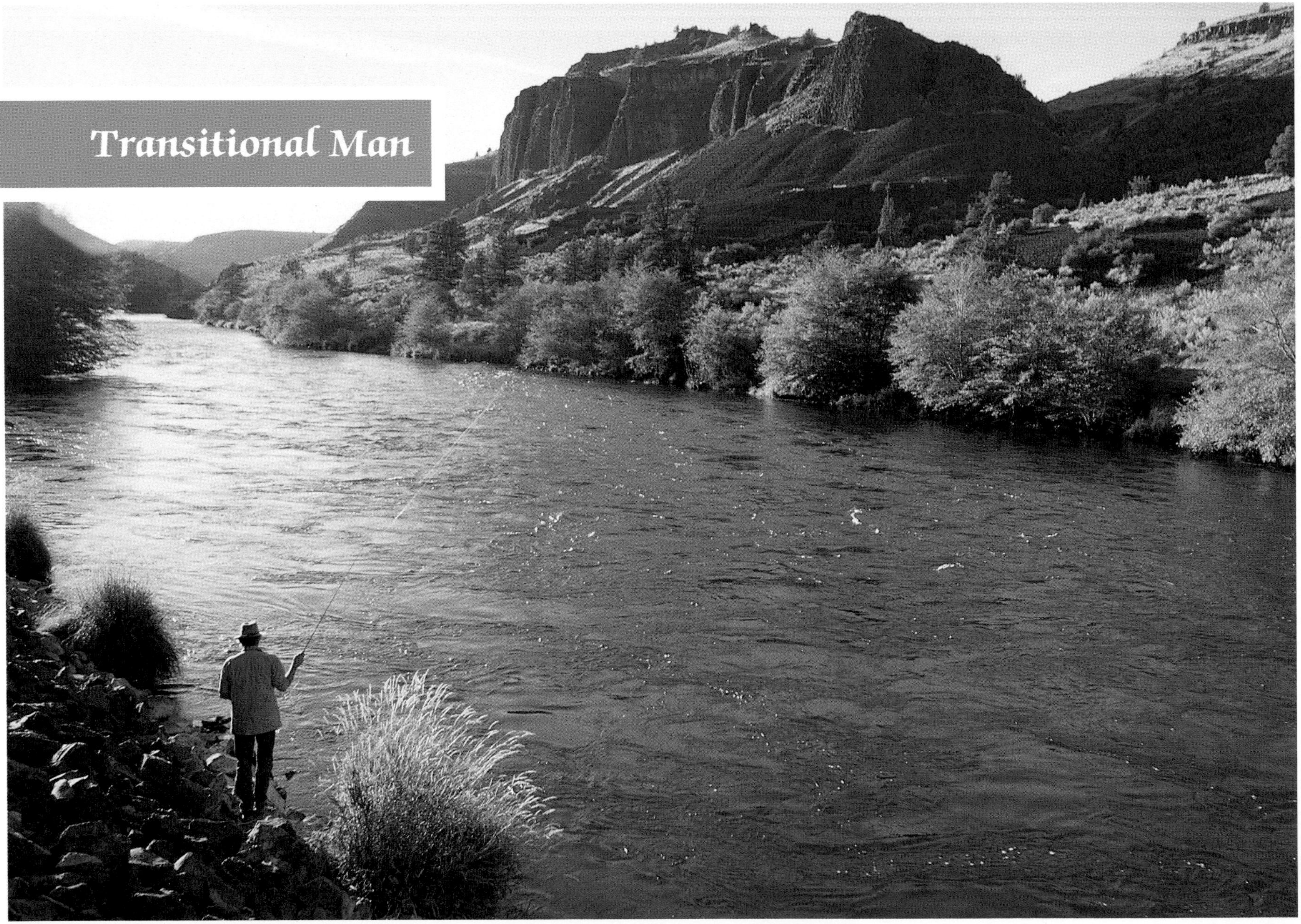

In the recent Ice Age the broad valleys of south-central Oregon, east of the Deschutes, captured runoff from the Cascade Mountains to the west and the fault-block mountains to the east. The resulting large lakes were actually inland seas. As these receded, in drier times after the Ice Age, hunters migrated into the basin, drawn by the teeming bird and mammal life gathered around the water, and by all the fish that swam in it.

These Indian hunters probably moved in from the east, across the Rockies: wandering tendrils of tribes from the Great Plains. There is also some speculation that they were members of Asian tribes who migrated directly from the Bering Straights bridge down the western half of the North American continent. Their route of arrival is in question; their eventual Asian origins, in either case, were the same.

The first record of man found in Oregon comes from Fort Rock Cave, on the Reub Long ranch north of Silver Lake. There is no water near it now; back then the cave overlooked a lake shore. Sandals made of sagebrush bark were among the artifacts discovered at Fort Rock in 1938. They have been radio-carbon dated at approximately 13,000 years before the present. The men who

wore them lived in a cave, but how primitive were they? Stones shaped to form sinkers were found along with the woven sandals. The stones were used to weight fishing nets, which were set in the lake, the waves of which lapped at the base of the slope beneath the entrance to the cave.

Arrowheads, scrapers, and other evidence of Indians have been found beneath the layer of ash that Mount Mazama scattered 6,600 years ago. The area that is now covered by Wickiup Reservoir was already well settled. The Mazama event was geologically recent, but old in terms of the tenure of man on the North American continent. Far more recent were the bleached remains of wickiup lodges, framed of willow and lodgepole pine, that still stood in meadows alongside the upper river when white men arrived. These frames gave Wickiup Reservoir its name.

By the time white men arrived, the lakes of the Fort Smith Basin had receded. Indians hunted seasonally there, but no longer lived in the area year around. But well-worn trails were beaten between the Klamath Basin, far in the south, across the entire interior plateau, for annual tribal movements to fishing sites on the Columbia River. Recall that the horse did not arrive until the Spanish explored the Southwest in the 1700s; all of the earlier evolutionary horses had died out on this continent long before early man crossed to it. So these annual Indian migrations were made on foot until the mid-1700s.

The remains of 29 Indian pit houses sprinkle an alluvial terrace overlooking the lower Deschutes River at Macks Canyon. They have been dated at about 2,000 years

before the present. These pit houses were 15 to 20 feet in diameter, built in excavated depressions, and roofed. A deep central area was surrounded by a shallower shelf, or bench. The circular center was the main domestic area; fire pits, and the remains of tools, have been found in that part of the houses. The bench surrounding the central area was used for sleeping and storage.

Above: *Wild roses brighten the brushy banks of the river in June and July.* RENA LANGILLE

Facing Page: *Long, broad, and deep runs typify the Deschutes. Lava headlands, such as those in the background, are exposed Columbia basalt flows, millions of years old.* JIM SCHOLLMEYER

Tools found at the Macks Canyon site include scrapers, knives, projectile points, drills, mortar and pestle, and milling stones. The record indicates that the Indians who lived there had an economy based on hunting, fishing, and gathering roots, greens, and berries. Bones were found from deer, antelope, rabbit, elk, bighorn sheep, beaver, coyote, and bobcat. Fish bones and mussel shells indicate the Indians looked to the Deschutes River for food. It is likely that they also migrated to the Columbia River sites, if not to fish, at least to trade with other Indians.

The first English-speaking visitation to the Deschutes River was made by the Lewis and Clark expedition, in late October of 1805. Lewis and Clark and their men were distracted by the twin problems of passing their canoes through the brutal chutes near Celilo Falls, and at the same time negotiating with the Indians gathered there. The party passed the mouth of the Deschutes River, gave it a preoccupied description and a name that didn't stick. But there isn't any evidence they went up it, or even took much notice of it.

Far more of the Lewis and Clark journals make note of their dealings with the Indians. Tribes gathered on the Columbia from many directions when the salmon ran. Estimates suggest that as many as 3,000 men, women, and children camped around the Celilo site, near the present town of The Dalles, to fish and to trade.

One Lewis and Clark journal description gives a hint at what living conditions might have been for the Indians at that time: "...we are nearly covered with fleas, which were so thick among the straw and fish skins at the upper part of the portage...that every man of the party was obliged to strip naked...that they might have an opportunity of brushing the fleas off their legs and bodies."

Not far down the river, Lewis and Clark met Indians who already spoke some English. They had been trading for years with men who came to the coast by ship, looking for furs.

John Jacob Astor's overland party, led by Wilson Hunt and headed in the same direction, to form what would soon become the town of Fort George, and later Astoria, dealt with the same Indians at the same place seven years after Lewis and Clark, in 1812. Hunt's notes were embellished in Washington Irving's slightly fanciful book "Astoria", and came out looking at the Indians this way:

Left: *The spring-fed Metolius River is one of the world's prettiest. It rises out of lava beds on the east slope of the Cascades, flows smoothly through ponderosa forests in its upper reaches, then gathers more springs, and more strength, before tipping into a canyon and plunging down to join the Deschutes.*
JIM SCHOLLMEYER

Right: *A small rainbow showing distinct parr marks down its sides. These markings, and its slender shape, identify it as a steelhead smolt on its migration downstream toward the ocean. In old photos of monstrous catches on the Deschutes, where trout were strung on wires and displayed proudly, a great part of the catch was always made up of these unfortunate smolts, taken from life before they got a chance to become five to fifteen pound returnees. In defense of those early anglers, the life cycle of the steelhead was not understood then, and they did not know about all the potential they killed.* BRIAN O'KEEFE

"Mr. Hunt found the inhabitants shrewder and more intelligent than any Indians he had met with. ...they were a community of arrant rogues and freebooters." Thieves and savages, he might have added. A few sentences later he did. It was the way the Indians were thought of by those who slowly accreted their world.

The Deschutes River got its eventual name from wandering French-Canadian trappers, who called it "La Rivere des Chutes", or 'the river of the rapids.' The name is not based on the violent nature of the Deschutes itself, but on the fact that it enters the Columbia River near "des Chutes" at Celilo. It is mildly disappointing to discover that the river of the rapids, which has an infinity of them, got its name for the rapids of another river, rapids that now lie stilled beneath a reservoir.

The first recorded journey into the Deschutes River country itself was made by Peter Skene Ogden. He was head of a trapping brigade, exploring for the Hudson's Bay Company, in December of 1825. He began at the mouth of the Deschutes River, on the Columbia River. His route took him through the hills to the west of the river, not up the course of the river itself.

Ogden descended to the river and camped at Dry Creek, just a few miles downstream from the present town of Warm Springs, nearly 100 miles above the mouth. His party crossed the winter-swollen river, losing four horses doing it, and moved out of the Deschutes canyon to the east, across the flats that now sport Madras.

Ogden was after furs, and had hunters out for game. His diaries record the daily sightings of deer and beaver, but note little about the land through which he traveled. He made no comment on the Deschutes River canyon, or any of its spectacular landmarks. The Ogden party nearly starved going up the Crooked River gorge, eating the few beaver they trapped, butchering a horse when they had to. They continued their explorations over the divide into the John Day country.

Ogden returned to the Deschutes a year later, but again crossed it to explore the regions beyond it. Trapping did not become much of a factor in the Deschutes River country itself.

Left: *Sherars Falls is a violent constriction of the river where it slices through a lava flow. Indians net steelhead and salmon there, from platforms that still look fragile, but are not nearly as hazardous as those from which their ancestors fished in exactly the same place and the same way for thousands of years. The falls is considered by boaters to be unrunnable, though it has been done, almost always with fatal or at least injurious results.* JIM SCHOLLMEYER

The region did not get busy with the comings and goings of white men until gold was discovered in the rivercourses around Canyon City, a town near John Day, in the early 1850s. By the 1860s, the rush got on. But the Deschutes hid little gold.

Unlike most western rivers, the Deschutes was a barrier to travel, not a way of travel. It was not a destination, but something in the way of getting to one. The primary route of travel was from The Dalles across the Deschutes to Canyon City, then on to Fort Harney, at what is now Burns, and on from there to the growing minefields at Orofino and other places in Idaho. Pack strings moved supplies to the mines, brought gold dust and ore back.

There were few good crossings between the mouth of the river and the entrance of the Crooked River, more than 100 miles upstream. One of the fords was 50 miles up, at Sherars Falls, where a basalt flow pinched the lower river. But it was dangerous. In 1860 John Y. Todd built a toll bridge at the site. It was highly successful, though Todd was too busy with other enterprises to bother building approach roads leading into or out of the canyon. His bridge became a link between two of the busiest cities in the Pacific Northwest, The Dalles and Canyon City. Millions of dollars worth of gold were carried across it.

In 1871 Joseph Sherar bought Todd's bridge. He paid attention to business, building approach roads on both sides of the canyon, and eventually constructed a three-story, 33-room tavern for travelers, called Sherar's Hotel. It became a major waystop on the most important route into Oregon's interior region, and was the busiest site on the river in its day. There is a modern bridge there now. A pair of blue fiberglass outhouses perch nakedly in the sun, on the same black Columbia River Basalt flow that pinches the river and causes Sherars Falls. Indians still net fish from precarious platforms hanging over the falls. The old hotel and the rest of the settlement are gone.

Small bands of Indians made raids on the miners who crossed the river and traveled the region. They pestered the few ranchers who tried to settle the land east of the river. Chief Paulina made the most trouble, and wrote the worst story, from the white man's point of view. Paulina was a renegade Snake Indian of the Walapi tribe, and was for a time called the Attila of the sagelands. He escaped so many firefights, in which so many around him were killed, that the peaceful Warm Springs Indians, his bitter enemies, believed he was bulletproof.

Paulina was coerced into attending a peace conference by the capture and holding of his wife. He signed an agreement in 1864, then turned around and immediately tried to make a massacre at Fort Klamath. He was driven off with substantial losses. Troops were sent after him, but Paulina outmaneuvered them constantly.

This was not a pleasant game of tit-for-tat; many people were killed on both sides. Paulina often raided Warm Springs territory on the Mount Jefferson side of the Deschutes, killing men, taking captives, and stealing horses. Paulina once surprised a small band of Warm Springs Indians, out on a hunt just east of the Deschutes. Though the Warm Springs raised a flag of truce, Paulina calculated their numbers, saw his were greater, then shot them up. One of their chiefs was killed.

Below: *Most Dolly Varden make meals of trout this size of this small Dolly. They are fish of the Deschutes headwaters, primarily the Metolius, and have been misnamed: they are actually bull trout.*
JIM SCHOLLMEYER

Many of the Warm Springs warriors finally enlisted with the white troops, serving as scouts to help track Paulina. But it was a tiny party of four men who finally hunted him down in April of 1867.

Paulina made a raid on the John Day River stage stop of James N. Clark, who escaped. The Indians burned Clark's buildings and made off with a band of his cattle. Clark rode to Antelope, another stage stop, and enlisted the help of Howard Maupin and two other men. They tracked Paulina and his men toward the Deschutes, and caught up with them at dawn in the gorge of Trout Creek. The indians were camped, eating a breakfast of freshkilled beef.

The four men opened fire from the rims on one side of the gorge. The Indians ran up the far rims, leaving Paulina behind, his hip smashed by a round from a Henry rifle.

Howard Maupin is credited with firing the fatal shot. Maupin later ran a ferry that crossed the Deschutes at the mouth of Bakeoven Creek. The current town at the site is named after him. For many years Maupin lived in a ranch house up Trout Creek, within sight of where he had killed Paulina. He kept the Indian's scalp nailed above the door until 1902, when the house burned down.

Paulina's bones were left to bleach in the sun where he fell in 1867. After his death the region was peaceful, open to settlement.

Below: *Almost any boulder that an angler can find a way to approach, in this case with a long cast from upstream, will reveal a trout that is willing to pounce on the fly, but reluctant to surrender to the rod.*
BILL MCMILLAN

The Railroad War

The story of the railroad's arrival in the Deschutes River canyon is almost as cataclysmic as the geological history of the river itself. When you boat the river today, hike along it, or fish it, evidence of what is called the "railroad war" will be visible all around you.

The laying of rails up the river was one of the most violent railroad projects in the history of the country. It seems to have focused in physical action energies pent-up from decades of previous railroad battles, most of which were won by political or financial intrigue, without noise of arms. Lots of noise was made in the Deschutes River Canyon; casualties were actually minor and few.

In 1855, half a century before the first spike was driven, an Army Engineers survey party under Lt. Henry Abbot declared that trains could not be brought up the narrow, rocky gorge. Abbot reported: "..the Deschutes Valley is mostly a barren region, furrowed by immense canyons, and offering very few inducements to settlers. Its few fertile spots...are separated from the rest of the world by almost impassable barriers, and nature seems to have guaranteed it forever to the wandering savage and the lonely seeker after the wild and sublime..."

Eastern timber supplies played out toward the end of the last century, 50 years after Abbot's announcement. Timber cruisers began to show up in the forests on the east slopes of the Cascade Mountains, in the Paulinas, and in the Ochocos. They found billions of board feet of timber ready to be felled. But where was the way to get it from the center of supply, Bend, to what Lt. Abbot had called "the rest of the world"? Rails were needed.

It was a time when the main trunk lines had already been built across the country. The railroad barons elbowed each other for the few remaining side shows into which they could poke their eager noses.

In 1900 the Columbia Southern Railroad had reached south from Biggs, on the Columbia River, to Shaniko, a few miles east of the Deschutes River and now one of Oregon's most famous ghost towns. But that railroad did not reach into the timber country, and it was not practical to extend it to Bend. Another route was needed.

Surveys made in the first years after the turn of the century made it clear that the only practical route into central Oregon was that impossible one right up the Deschutes River. The gorge route formed a gateway to all of that timber. It was also an opening for extensions of the line into California, or into the eastern part of Oregon, which thrived with mining at the time. But forests were the sleeping giants that enticed the barrons into their quarrel.

In February of 1906 the Oregon Trunk Line was formed, and became a subsidiary of the James J. Hill empire, which included the Great Northern Line. Edward H. Harriman, of the Union Pacific Line, entered the race through a subsidiary called the DesChutes Railroad. Both filed for nearly the same route up the river, at nearly the same time.

Above: *As ugly as its job, the turkey vulture cleans up carrion, and is often seen high above the river.* WORTH MATHEWSON

Facing page: *The canyon of the lower Deschutes is cut so sharply because it is relatively young: the river has had only three to four million years to erode its course since the uplifting Cascade Mountains turned it north toward the Columbia River.* RANDY STETZER

In 1906 a wealthy and avid sportsman showed up on the river. He traveled for months, visited the few ranches already established in the canyon, and pronounced the fishing marvelous. He bought options on a few pieces of land to improve his own future access to the river. Then he disappeared. When the truth leaked out he was discovered to be engineer John F. Stevens, builder of the Panama Canal, hired by James J. Hill to secure some strategic easements along the Deschutes for the coming railroad. Through such skulduggery, combined with better building, Hill and his Oregon Trunk Line were able to win the subsequent war.

It started with a skirmish in 1909, when both camps prepared to begin contruction. Harriman crews of the DesChutes Railroad built their own supply road for wagons down Harris Canyon, to the river on the east bank, 12 miles upstream from the Columbia. They made camp on a riverside flat and prepared to go to work. Oregon Trunk Line crews, under Harry Carleton, forced their way down the Harris Canyon road at night, in a noisy firefight that failed to injure anybody. They announced camp on the same flat.

Left: *The structure of the river is visible where it flows north around the farms at Kaskela: the long deep runs with even currents, and frequent riffles and rapids where the young river cuts down through another basaltic lava flow. The Warm Springs Indian Reservation, and the foothills of the Mutton Mountains, are on the far side. The mountains are named for wild sheep that roamed the slopes before domestic sheep brought diseases that wiped them out.* DAVE HUGHES

A stalemate followed for a few weeks, with no construction getting done. The Oregon Trunk financial folks broke the deadlock by sneaking in and buying a ranch at the head of Harris Canyon. They blockaded the road the other company had built, cutting off supply wagons heading down to feed the DesChutes Railroad crews.

The sheriff and a judge rode out and ordered the Oregon Trunk men to move. They refused. The result was a scuffle in which the judge was tumbled around in the dust. The Oregon Trunk Line was ordered to remove itself to the west side of the river and stay there; the DesChutes Railroad folks were ordered to keep to the east side. Construction began on both sides of the river in the middle of the night on July 26, 1909. The race was on.

Work in the tight and hot canyon of the Deschutes River came at the end of an era. It was nearly the last major construction project done entirely by hand. DesChutes Railroad bosses made an early attempt to use power. They dismantled a massive steamshovel, lowered it over the canyon walls piece by piece, and reassembled it along the river. The effort proved useless; the canyon walls of hard basaltic rock could not be broken up by the power equipment of that day.

Construction became a matter of hand-drilling holes in the lava cliffs, charging the holes with black powder, and blasting sections of rock. Rubble was removed by pick, shovel, and wheelbarrow. When the bed was ready, ties and rails were also laid by hand.

The Oregon Trunk Line employed more than 3,000 men, the DesChutes Railroad

Above: *A steelhead this bright has just made its run in from the ocean, and probably hurried doing it. This one has a wildness to it, measured in the sharp angles of its untattered fins; it has never seen a hatchery pen. Regulations on the river require that wild steelhead be released to spawn, which makes sense: the river needs their wild genetics. Natural fish, while being about equal in numbers with those from hatcheries in the total run, are more aggressive, take flies and lures more often, and make up far more than half of the catch. If all fish were to be kept, hatchery steelhead would quickly become dominant. The fish that the river and time devised would soon become extinct.* LEWIS ROSER

Right: *It is the author's habit to wander through bankside brush and grasses on windless dawns, snooping into little lives with a camera and close-up lens. That is when beauty can be caught napping.*
DAVE HUGHES

nearly 4,000. Most of them were immigrants from southern Europe, many of them Italian. It took 15,000 pounds of beef daily to feed the crews. Each contruction company kept its own herd of cattle on the hillsides above the canyon. Many nights, gangs would cross the river and frighten the cattle, stampeding them so the rival crew had to go hungry. A lot of the "war" consisted of such harrassments.

Above: *The long drop down to the river through rolling rocks, rattlesnakes, and poison oak: any place where access requires effort and an element of caution, the fishing is likely to be lonely once the river is reached.* SCOTT RIPLEY

Facing page: *A wild summer steelhead that has been back in its native river long enough to regain some of the natural characteristics of the redband strain of rainbow, which gives resident trout the name "redsides."* FRANK AMATO

The smoke from one black powder blast settled to reveal a ball of writhing rattlesnakes, their winter den shattered. That night men rowed boats silently across the river. They left burlap sacks awakening next to the other company's warm wood stoves.

DesChutes gangs sweated through a long day, laying a perfect stretch of rails in a narrow stretch of the canyon. Oregon Trunk powder monkeys stayed up all that night, blasting. In the morning the DesChutes men woke to find their new rails buried by rubble and rock, thrown clear across the river.

Construction camps were intentionally built exactly at the river's edge whenever it was possible. If they were placed higher up, the opposing crew would cross at night and ignite the dry grass below camp. Fire would rush up the hill.

Such skirmishes sound playful in retrospect. They were not. Rifle fire crossed the river at night. One day a boulder rolled down onto an Oregon Trunk Line worktrain, without casualties, but with retaliation. That night a DesChutes Railroad watchman found a lit fuse in the middle of camp. He stamped it out, then trailed it to a full keg of black powder. Had it detonated, it would have caused casualties. A lot of DesChutes workers pulled out the next day, and time was lost while replacements were found.

Each side employed spotters on the canyon rims. Their job was to watch where the other company stored its powder. On moonless nights, bands of men would slip across and set it off.

The battle ran for 50 miles up the river. The climax came where the tag end of the Mutton Mountains cross the river, at the current site of North Junction. Oregon Trunk Line crews on the west bank ran into a rock wall that they could not blast away or tunnel through. They needed to cross to the other side. That was a problem; they had made themselves unwelcome there.

A rancher who owned the property at that point on the river got caught in the quarrel between the armed camps. The federal government stepped in and enforced an agreement calling for a 999-year cease fire and joint track usage in the next 12 miles. At the end of those 12 miles the two crews parted. The DesChutes Railroad built its track out of the canyon at Trout Creek. The Oregon Trunk Line continued construction up the river for another 10 miles before leaving it to climb out at Willow Creek, just upstream from the town of Warm Springs. The war was over.

Mecca Flat, just downstream from Warm Springs, was the last Oregon Trunk Line construction camp in the canyon. It got its name because the men were exhausted from the hard labor and constant fighting. They knew that when the rails reached Mecca the most difficult and dangerous work would be behind them.

The battle of the gorge was essentially won long before it was over, and not by anything that happened in the canyon. In 1909, the same year that construction began down near the mouth of the river, the Central Oregon Railroad was formed. It filed for a route from Madras to Bend, usurping the only good crossing over the Crooked River. In 1910, while the race raged in the canyon, Hill's Oregon Trunk Line bought out the new

Above: *This cabin above Dant was the headquarters of a homesteader who finally relinquished it. It is now the weekend cabin of a fisherman who reaches it by rowing his drift boat across the river.* FRANK AMATO

Facing page: *Dillion Falls, not far from Bend on the upper river, is a sudden interruption in an otherwise fairly placid stretch of stream.* TOM BUGLIONE

company, with its rights to the Crooked River crossing. He began contruction at that end of the line, on the plateau, while rail was still being laid toward it from the other end. This maneuver blocked Harriman's attempt to build a parallel line on the flatlands, once he got his road out of the canyon. It no longer mattered who won the race in the gorge. The two lines would share the same crossing over the Crooked River.

The span across the Crooked was a wonder in its time. It was 350 feet long, and one of the highest bridges in the world, standing 320 feet above the river.

On October 5, 1911, James J. Hill drove a symbolic golden spike at the end of his railroad, in Bend. There were no sawmills large enough to supply anything but local lumber needs at the time rails arrived. But in a few years the mills were built, the timber knocked down and cut up, and the boards hauled down the river and delivered profitably to the rest of the world.

For 16 years Hill's Great Northern Line did not extend the rails beyond Bend. Then he executed his final plan for the line up the Deschutes River, making it a link in the trunk line to California. The first train ran the entire distance from the Columbia River to California in 1928.

Oregon Trunk Line men had laid better track, with a more consistent grade, in the canyon. Through the following years Harriman's Union Pacific Line capitulated bits of track here and there. The whole line was finally consolidated to a single track, called the Oregon Trunk Line, at midcentury. Present day trains run the west bank from the mouth of the river up to North Junction, where the Mutton mountains force a crossing. Trains depart eastward from the river on the old DesChutes Railroad grade up Trout Creek, then toot through the town of Gateway on their way toward Bend.

The railroad war lasted two years. In the end, after the consolidation, it meant nothing. But to this day it has great meaning to people who visit the river for recreation.

Abandoned grade forms the seven mile foot path on the east bank between Warm Springs and Trout Creek. The gravel road eight miles upstream from Maupin to the Deschutes Club locked gate was built on the old DesChutes River Railroad bed. Fourteen miles of private road on Club property, to North Junction, were also laid over the abandoned bed.

The paved road downstream from Maupin to Sherars Falls, on the east bank, is owed to the railroad war. Twenty-eight miles of rough BLM road follows the river from Sherars Falls to Macks Canyon, on DesChutes Railroad lines. Twenty-three miles of level trail run from Macks Canyon to the mouth of the river, most on abandoned railroad bed, for the ambitious who like to hike.

The existing railroad, with its snorting trains, and the abandoned grades, which became roads and trails, are major features you will encounter constantly in the canyon today.

It is interesting to note that the tracks leave the river canyon not far below the point where the two geographies, those of the upper and lower rivers, meet. The volcanic flows that torture the course of the upper river forced both of the arrogant barons to carry their rails out of the canyon.

Changes Man Has Made

The visible source of the Deschutes River is at the outlet of Little Lava Lake, in the mile-high timber country just off Century Drive, about 25 miles southwest of Bend. In high-water years an open channel brings water down from Lava Lake to Little Lava, but most years that channel is dry. It is suspected that underground systems deliver water all the way from Elk Lake, 15 miles farther north, through Lava Lake, and into the Deschutes via Little Lava. Elk Lake could therefore be the invisible source; but there are probably hundreds of those.

For 20 miles from its visible source, the river runs south, gathering feeders and springs. It is small, cold, and bright over its clean pebbled bottom. Willow and jack pine crowd it.

Then it enters the long stretches that were once prairies: Crane Prairie, named for the long-necked and patiently peering birds that hunted tadpoles and frogs on the broad meadows, and Wickiup Prairie, named for the bleached frames of shelters the Indians left there.

The Deschutes makes its turn east and then north in the prairies that are no longer bemeadowed, then flows 30 miles through jack pine timber and grazing meadows to Bend. Along the way it plunges over Pringle, Benham, and Dillon falls. It gathers the Little Deschutes, Fall River, and Spring River. Throughout this mileage the peaceful Deschutes River stores its potential floods in deposits of porous lava rock.

From Bend the river enters the new canyon it gouged out of the 1,000-year old Newberry Crater volcanic flows. The bed tilts steeply; at one time the river thundered over cataract and cataract for 45 miles, picking up at the lower end of this reach both the Metolius and Crooked rivers. This is the area of sharp edges, of rock that hasn't had time to erode. The end of this reach is the end of the upper river, the end of the new geology.

Below the junction of the two large tributaries, the Deschutes River enters the 3-million year old canyon cut through Columbia River Basalt flows. It flows straight north; its features are rugged and spectacular, but the nature of the canyon is relatively constant. The river flows through this canyon for 100 miles, picking up the Warm Springs River, White River, and a few minor tributaries along the way. The Deschutes River enters the Columbia River just upstream from the town of The Dalles. The two waters meet placidly now, in the lake behind The Dalles Dam.

The Deschutes gains most of its water from the east slopes of the Cascade Mountains. The Crooked River is the only major tributary arising on the eastern plateau. Because of the great lava sponge in the upper river, at one time the Deschutes had the most constant and uniform flow of any river of comparable size in the country.

It is man's nature to bring water to land. The first settlers in central Oregon, in the last

Above: *A single chukar can out-cackle a barnyard full of roosters. Imported from India, beginning in the late 1950s, this hardy partridge filled an arid niche that was almost empty of gamebirds. Chukar are plump and pigeon-sized, and one of the best of all birds on the table.* MARGARET THOMPSON MATHEWSON

Facing page: *Whenever the land was level and near water, homesteaders built approximate houses and outbuildings, and tried to coax a living out of the ungenerous soil. A few of these benches are still farmed, but most were too small: it takes a lot of acres in sage country to provide the means for a good life.* ANDY ANDERSON

decades of the 1800s, built their cabins on flats in small stream valleys. Almost immediately they devised ways to divert some of the streamflow over the parched flats to water kitchen vegetable patches and a few fruit trees. As early as the summer of 1904, Deschutes River water began to flow through the Pilot Butte Canal, at Bend. Redmond was still a city of tents and rough board shanties when Deschutes water reached it by way of canal in 1906.

When Madras was settled, on the vast flats above the rim of the canyon, it was evident what water would do if applied to its rich soils. By 1913 agriculture had already become important there, and irrigation water from the Deschutes canals was available seasonally. But maximum river runoff came in spring and early summer. The water supply was inadequate in late summer when demand was highest. An application was entered to use 400,000 acre feet of Deschutes water annually for irrigation in the Madras area. This was the start of a 30 year effort to dam and divert the river.

Construction of small and crude dams to back up the water began in the 1920s. In 1921 the Bureau of Reclamation began to plan for two reservoirs on the upper river.

Crane Prairie Reservoir was the first component of what came to be called the Deschutes Project. Crane Prairie was built as a rock-fill dam in 1922, funded by irrigation districts in the Madras area. Waters flooded the old prairie where cranes once hunted, and large parts of the forest around it. In order to recover the better timber, the reservoir was drained and raised again. Stands of jack pine were left uncut; they stand stark and thick in the reservoir to this day, perches and nests for osprey and their young. The orginal 1922 dam leaked; it was rebuilt by the Bureau of Reclamation in 1939 and 1940.

Work started on Wickiup Dam in 1939, using Civilian Conservation Corps laborers put out of work by the depression. Construction was interrupted by World War II, and was not completed until 1949. Wickiup flooded the great meadows that once attracted deer and elk, and the Indians who hunted them.

Crane Prairie and Wickiup reservoirs are giant water storage tanks for the irrigation districts near Bend, Redmond, and Madras. Water is gathered in winter and spring, released in summer and fall, solving that problem nature has of applying water to soil at the wrong time. Released water is diverted just above Bend, into a canal that is the next major link in the Deschutes Project. From there

Left: *Crane Prairie was flooded before its lodgepole pines were logged. Dead trees stand in forests today just as they did before the dam was built. Channels that are the old streambed of the Deschutes and its feeders now wind through the dead pines as pathways for boats and float tubes that cruise the waters in search for lunker brown and rainbow trout.* JIM SCHOLLMEYER

it flows through more than 200 miles of main canals, then into 700 miles of ditches, which are the last link in the system.

The result of irrigation diversion is an upper Deschutes that is a remnant of what the river once was. Crane Prairie and Wickiup reservoirs are great fisheries, and put out some of Oregon's largest trout every season. But, as many stream fishermen and rafters have noted, a lake is not a river.

From Wickiup Dam downstream for 40 miles to Bend, the river is placid, averaging two miles per hour, with few rapids. Unstable flows in this part of the river, caused by irrigation needs, have reduced trout fishing to put-and-take. At one time there was an excellent population of brown trout here, some of them large. But siltation of spawning beds has reduced them to a point where the fishing is of marginal quality.

The river is nearly dewatered below the diversion canal at Bend. Until you reach the beginning of the lower river, 50 miles downstream, it is too low to float from April until October. The water is too high to fish effectively when water is allowed to pass the diversion. It is too low to fish when water is removed, and what little stream is left is shallow and beaten by the summer sun. Warm water drives even the brown trout deep into the few pools left.

It is not commonly recognized that the reduced flow of the upper river itself contributes only 20 percent of the flow of the large and boisterous lower river. The spring-fed Metolius River, rushing from the ponderosa pine country west of the river, provides 40 percent. Crooked River, meandering out of the mountains and across the dry lands to the east of the river, adds another 40 percent. These enter from their opposite sides just a few miles apart, about 10 miles from Madras.

Below: *A heron crouches in the shallows, its long neck withdrawn. Herons have spear-like bills for piercing careless chub, small trout, or reckless steelhead smolts.*
WORTH MATHEWSON

Left: *A drift boat maneuvers toward the slot that is the only safe entrance into Buckskin Mary rapids. Their ride is about to turn bumpy.* FRANK AMATO

Its main attraction is the great plug of lava, 800 feet high, left when the Crooked and Deschutes Rivers eroded new channels around each side of Newberry Crater flows of a thousand years ago.

Simtustus and Lake Billy Chinook are narrow and deep, formed by filling the Deschutes gorge where it worked into lava flows. Crane Prairie and Wickiup are broad and shallow, formed as they are by filling the old meadows that once spread alongside the upper river. The irrigation reservoirs are rich in aquatic insect life — food for trout — and have excellent fishing. The power reservoirs are relatively food-poor in their darker depths, and do not offer much chance at numbers of trout, or trophy trout. They do offer excellent kokanee and smallmouth bass fishing.

The four dams that now exist on the river are likely the last that will ever be built. Eleven proposals for new hydro power projects appeared in the late 1970s and early 1980s. The Coalition for the Deschutes was formed to fight them. The Coalition was able to force a study of the projects. Public hearings were packed with protesters. The study itself proved unfavorable to development. The state legislature passed a bill forbidding any hydro project that would kill a single anadromous fish, or that would reduce any wild trout fishery to dependence on a hatchery. Further hydroelectric generation on the Deschutes River is effectively dead.

Both of these major tributaries now enter the Deschutes as arms of Lake Billy Chinook, pent up behind Round Butte Dam. This was the second of two power dams built where the upper and lower rivers meet.

The first power project was Pelton Dam, completed in 1958 by Portland General Electric. It holds back Simtustus Reservoir. The dam is 200 feet high; the lake behind it is seven miles long. With the construction of Round Butte Dam immediately upstream, Pelton Dam now serves as both a power facility and a reregulating dam, or surge basin, stabilizing releases from Round Butte dam above it.

Round Butte Dam was completed in 1964, also by Portland General Electric. It is 440 feet high, and backs up the main Deschutes for eight miles, as well as capturing the Metolius and Crooked Rivers in its east and west arms. The Cove Palisades State Park sits astride the Crooked and Deschutes arms.

The final major change has been along the lower river. As the two sets of tracks left from the railroad war were consolidated into one track in the 1920s and 1930s, many miles of abandoned bed were converted into automobile road in the 1940s and 1950s. Most of this was done by the Bureau of Land Management, but some was done by private ranchers and other owners.

About 40 miles of river directly downstream from Pelton Dam, and about 25 more miles from the mouth of the river upstream, are still unroaded, or roaded but with vehicle access closed to the public. The old railroad grade, and in some places the active track itself, serve as hiking trails thoughout this entire mileage. Thirty-five miles of active road are open to the public in the lower river, in the center reach of it, from a few miles above Maupin downstream to Mack's Canyon. Only seven miles of this are paved; the rest is graveled, and it will bounce you around.

In the mid-1960s, BLM proposed to build a road between Warm Springs and South Junction, the first 13 miles of the lower river, below the power dams. At the time there was point access at those two places, and another access between them at the Trout Creek Campground. You could reach the river, but if you wanted to move along it, you hiked or floated in a boat.

Herb Lundy, a senior editor at the Oregonian newspaper and a dedicated fisherman, took up the matter of the road by writing a letter directly to Stewart Udall, then Secretary of the Interior, telling him that the road would degrade the river. Lundy wrote that,

"Motor traffic, campgrounds and drive-and-fish anglers would quickly convert this now relatively secluded section of the river into a put-and-take river supported by hatchery plants."

On 24 May, 1967, Udall issued an order that no road would be built. It is celebrated in the simple and rusted steel plaque, on a steel stake driven into the rocky soil at Trout Creek, that quotes Udall: "We will be remembered for the roads we did not build."

Current social values, and the recent act barring further dams, make it unlikely that man will cause much more disruption on the Deschutes River, at least in the foreseeable future.

Below: *The Pelton Re-regulating Dam, just upstream from Warm Springs, levels out the flow of the lower river, much as the upstream lava aquifer used to do it before the irrigation impoundments were built.*
JIM SCHOLLMEYER

Brushes With Wild Things

People have specialties. Some can identify every wildflower they find peeking from beneath a streamside sage. Others can name rocks, and recognize their volcanic or sedimentary origins. Birds are a favorite. On an early trip to the Deschutes, my Dad heard the harsh call of a bird from a nearby hillside. The bird itself was not in sight.

Dad lifted his head, listened to the call again, then said, "That's a shrike."

We crossed through the dry scrub and flushed the bird from its low perch. "I was right," Dad said when he saw it. Later he showed me a picture of the bird in a book. It was exactly what he said it was.

Dad had never seen a shrike before.

His specialty is birds. He had studied the shrike's description, and read of its strident call. On hearing it, he recognized what he had read about. He considers it a waste of time when I study aquatic insects. "You should be learning about the birds," he tells me.

"Trout don't eat birds," I tell him back.

I won't try to tell you here how to identify aquatic insects, which are what I know the most about. Nor will I try to tell you how to identify wildflowers, birds, and terrestrial insects, which are what I know least about. I'll just recount some encounters I've had with some of them along the banks of the Deschutes, and let you study the guidebooks to whatever interests you most. I do recommend it: knowing the salient birds, insects, wildflowers, and plants will enhance your enjoyment of the river and the country that surrounds it.

On one of my first camping trips to the river, at South Junction, I woke earlier than my friends and went for a dawn walk, which is my habit. I headed up the rough dirt road toward the farms at Kaskela, rested from a good sleep, lifting my hiking boots high. I hadn't gone a mile before a strange crayfish halted my walk by scuttling through the dust between my feet. I kneeled to examine it. It was about two inches long, half of which was an angry-looking tail arched high over its back. Its pincer claws looked just like those of a crab the size of a half-dollar.

I had never seen such a thing, but like Dad with his shrike, I had no trouble deciding it was a scorpion. I carried a camera with a macro lense. I took a long range picture of the critter, then began edging up on it, refocusing and snapping as I moved ever nearer. The scorpion held still, posing broadside as the sun came up to light it, all the time holding that wicked tail poised over its back. Soon the critter filled the camera frame.

Suddenly the scorpion turned toward the camera, and charged possibly an inch or two. Its movements were magnified by the macro lense. I dropped the camera in panic and jumped backwards a yard or two. The scorpion, its bluff accomplished, scuttled on across the road and disappeared among the rocks on the other side. I gathered my camera and myself and continued my own morning stroll.

The sting of a scorpion can be fatal. But the species along the Deschutes only grows to about two inches long, and lacks the punch of larger species. They hunt insects and spiders at night, and hide by day in the cool shelter of rocks. I've never seen another on the river. Nor have I ever put my boots on in the morning without tipping them up and giving them a good shake.

On a recent float trip my fishing friends and I stopped off at a campsite above the Trout Creek access. That afternoon Richard Bunse came trotting back from a purposeful visit. "There's a black widow got its web spun in the upper left corner of the outhouse," he told us. Next time up, I took a look. It was a

Above: *Female spider stands guard over the silken egg-mass she has woven so carefully throughout the night in the cusp of the author's sunglasses.* DAVE HUGHES

Facing page: *A single shaft of sunlight ignites a morning mist.* MARGARET MITCHELL

Above: *An import not everybody is happy about; thistle crowns are pretty but warn you away.*
RENA LANGILLE

female black widow, though I confess I failed to turn it over to confirm the red hourglass on its abdomen. It's web was a compact wad of white silk, and appeared to be an egg mass guarded by the spider. I left her alone, and she left me alone. That's the way it works best.

Black widows are big spiders, and venomous. Their bite is painful but rarely fatal. The are shy, and will retreat unless driven into a corner, which was where that one started.

Another spider, large but harmless, took charge of my sunglasses one night. I'd left them out on a wooden grub box overnight. When I got up in the morning a female spider had laid her eggs in the concavity of one lens, then patiently spun layer after layer of silk over them. It was the pure white of a bride's gown, so transparent the eggs could be seen deep inside it. The spider, a beautiful creature itself, protectively straddled its work, its body in the center of the lens over the silk. Its legs, radiating out like the spokes of a wheel, were so long they spanned half the lens.

Ant lions live along the Deschutes. Look for their depressions in the dry sand around the bases of juniper trees, right in camp. The traps are only two or three inches across, an inch or two deep. They are perfectly shaped cones. When you find one, look for a colony of them nearby. Ant lions are beetle larvae; you won't see them, but roll a pebble into the pit and you will see the sand get excited, flicking and shifting. Poke around and dig the insect out if you like. I haven't. I'm sure it's ugly, and can pinch.

The first time I found a colony of ants attending aphids, in the high leaves of a gray sage alongside the river, I got excited about it. I've seen several of the colonies since, and suspect if you keep your eyes open you'll come across a colony, too. The aphids eat the sage leaves, the ants guard the aphids and milk their secretions; that's the way I understand it. However it works, I've gotten close enough to see that these are red ants, their mandibles look fierce, and they get restless when they know you are snooping around. They come right up on the tip ends of sage leaves, wiggling ther antennae furiously, trying to get at you. I wouldn't want to get them on me, but it's fun to watch them defending their aphids.

Fishing partner Jim Schollmeyer and I fished a shallow Deschutes sidecurrent once, just below Warm Springs. We were in the water but tight against the bank. Some short alders stood right at our backs, making us lift our backcasts high. My eye caught a rush of movement and I heard swift sound straight above me, 15 feet up. I jerked my head that way in time to see a detonation of feathers. A hawk flew off. Though I had seen it happen, all I had was a complication of impressions.

"What was that?" I asked Jim.

"A hawk caught a sparrow," he said.

Feathers glided down around us.

It was a small hawk, a sharp-shinned or a coopers. Larger red-tailed hawks hunt above the river, too, sailing high, their broad tails spread. Sometimes you can see the red on the backs of their tails when they wheel.

Golden eagles soar higher, almost always at a distance, up against the highest rims of the canyon. Their wingspan is up to eight feet, though most are smaller. They ride thermals and search the ground below for rabbits, rodents, carrion or snakes.

Red-winged blackbirds nest and scold in the alders at streamside. Meadowlarks perch on sage tops and call musically across the camp flats. Magpies come to quarrel over whatever food you might leave in camp. Toss out an extra pancake or slice of bread; they will come cautiously, peering and pecking.

Cliff swallows build their nests on the rock walls, and swarm low over the river whenever an insect hatch happens. They are a sign that fishing is about to get good.

Mergansers perch on stranded logs or gravel bars, taking off when you get too close, flying upstream or down in low and tight military formations. They take a tithe of steelhead and small trout. Kingfishers take the small fish, too, from hides on limbs directly over the water. Or they hover over shallows with quick wingbeats, then plunge to arise empty, or with a fish pinched in their strong beaks.

Right: *Shallow backchannels behind islands are excellent water for trout.* ANDY ANDERSON

Osprey are not common on the river, but last year, while floating quietly in a raft above South Junction, I spotted one flying up the river toward me. It was 100 feet high and a couple of hundred yards short of me when it did not interrupt its flight, or even pause, but suddenly stooped, exploded into the water, and emerged turning a trout in its talons. The wingspan of an osprey is between four and six feet. Nobody who has ever seen one in the moment that is fatal to a fish would begrudge an osprey the few trout it might take.

Canada geese nest along the river. They lead their yellow and clumsy flocks of fluff disdainfully away from the river, to browse or loaf in the sage, when boat traffic gets too heavy. Jet boat traffic on the bottom half of the lower river disturbs them, and has reduced the number of geese that nest there now.

Chukars are an import from India, brought over as gamebirds in the 1950s. They thrive in the steep and rocky Deschutes canyon. Their calling is reminiscent of chickens, but one or two of them could outshout a barnyard full of boastful roosters. Hunters with legs strong enough to dare the slopes do well on them. No bird tastes better.

I carry binoculars on my dawn walks. Seldom do I fail to spot at least a few mule deer high on the ridges above the river. Their long ears are always uplifted. Though I search for them far in the distance, they have always spotted me first. There are bobcats in the canyon, though I have never seen one. They eat

Below: An osprey tends its nest atop a telephone pole near the river. LEWIS ROSER

Below: An osprey tends its nest atop a telephone pole near the river. LEWIS ROSER

more jackrabbits than deer, which is also true of the coyotes that complain at dawn and dusk around the canyon rims.

If you travel the river enough, you will spot wild mink looping along the shore. Muskrats swim the eddied edges, always trailing rushes or reeds that they deliver to dens tucked under the banks.

Otter are not common on the river, but they cover lots of water, and it's not rare to see them. I fished a long choppy run for steelhead one evening; light was almost gone. A limb went by, only its end out of water, floating right down the center of the chop. It went under. Another came up nearby. Soon there were half a dozen of these limbs popping up and down, riding the current, shooting down the run. They were almost out of sight before I realized what they were: a family of otters, raising their heads out of the water to peer at me, trying to figure out what I was.

You'll see beaver if you keep quiet along the alder edges at evening. They'll be working, swimming twigs to where they want them. They won't be trying to dam the Deschutes. I taught fly fishing at a school on the river one summer. One of my students intentionally took a cast and hooked a beaver in the hide, a sin for which he would have paid with his expensive fly line had his leader not popped when his backing was nearly gone. I had to scold the student, though the beaver had already humbled him.

Poison oak is not a rumor along the river. It is there, though it crouches low, hiding in the grasses and bushes. It is one of the wild things I have brushed against. There is no sign that the poison oak regrets it.

I do. At one time I was not allergic to the stuff. In the Army, on a camouflage training course in California, I decorated my helmet with it. The drill sergeant laughed. I did, too. I wasn't bothered by it at all. You develop a sensitivity to the poison of this plant, sometimes slowly, and some people not at all. I've developed mine.

Poison oak grows as a shrub from a foot to 10 feet high. It travels singly, in thin rows or scattered clumps, and sometimes in thickets. It has three smooth and shiny leaves that are dark green in spring and summer, withering and turning red or yellow in fall. Its flowers are small, yellowish green, and come in clusters. It has grayish-white berries that shrivel but hang on through autumn and into winter. The stem of the plant keeps its bite even when its leaves are gone.

Poison oak deposits an oil on you when you touch it. You don't have any idea it's there until about three days later, when a rash begins to pop up. The rash forms where you touched the leaves or stem of the plant; often it comes up in a line on your forearm or leg, where you brushed along it. By the time the rash comes up, it's too late to do much but keep it covered with cortizone cream, and try not to scratch, which can spread it.

Above: A porcupine caught creeping to the water for a sip takes up its natural defense: a posture that erects its hidden quills. JIM SCHOLLMEYER

Right: *Some big brown trout lurk in the dappled waters of the middle and upper Deschutes. By the time they reach this size they become piscavores at least in part: making a portion of their living hunting smaller fish, including an occasional trout.* SCOTT RIPLEY

The last time I had poison oak, which was last year, which means I still haven't learned to stay out of it, I scratched until it got infected. My arm swelled up like a sausage, which was strange. I thought it was from the poison oak, but I finally went to a doctor and he told me the swelling was from the infection.

Poison oak rash lasts 10 days to two weeks. If you have it bad, go to the doctor without waiting. He can help ease you through it.

The best way to prevent poison oak is to learn to recognize it and stay away from it. If you are an overeager fisherman, and a fish rises along a bank that is sprinkled with it, staying away from it doesn't always work. The next best thing is to wash vigorously with pumice soap as soon as you can after you have the slightest hint you've been exposed to it. My policy now, when on the Deschutes, is to use the soap every evening, even if I've just seen poison oak going by in the distance. I don't trust it. Once I got it on my hands when I took off my wading boots at the end of the day. The oil had stuck to the leather. Now I wash my boots, too. Use the soap in a bucket, well back from the banks, and dump it where it won't pollute the water.

I am more frightened by poison oak than I am by rattlesnakes, though I confess the fright comes on more slowly with the plant than it does the snake. Most people I know get twitchy the second they see a snake. It's an instinct.

Most snakes along the river are not rattlesnakes. It's more common to see a bull snake, also called a gopher snake. They are tan to brown, slender, and have narrow heads. They are harmless, though they will give you a fright when they whip away. Garter snakes are also found along the river, and they have the same kind of movement.

Rattlesnakes are more dignified. They move more slowly. To me, their movement is not as sinister, though that's not a smart way to view the situation, since the rattlers have fangs and the other snakes don't.

I once viewed a rattlesnake in an interesting way. I was about to kneel to a spring, for a drink. A head appeared from under a rock, right where my nose would have gone. I was young then, not yet familiar with the triangular, blocky shape of the rattlesnake's

Below: *This is usually the way you'll see one—or more likely not see it: cryptic and unobtrusive, staying out of your way so long as you stay out of its way.* JIM SCHOLLMEYER

head. I dismissed this fellow as a bull snake; I continued to kneel though I withdrew my nose. I watched as the head went across the spring, disappeared under another rock, then tugged a tail after it. When I saw the tail I stood up, backed away, and found another place to drink.

Rattlesnakes sense vibrations. If you would rather not encounter them, carry a staff and thud the ground with it as you walk. Snakes will scatter, and you will never see them. I retract that; never say never. You will see fewer of them.

Deschutes rattlesnakes are prairie rattlers, seldom though sometimes achieving four feet in length. Most often they are about two feet long. They are brown, with light markings on their backs, and rather thick bodies for their size. They stay in the shade or underground during the heat of the day, sun themselves on sand or rocks mornings and evenings. They hunt small rodents such as mice and chip-munks, and are hunted themselves by eagles, hawks, and man. It's all right for the birds, but not for us. A rattlesnake should not be killed unless it is in a threatening position, and cannot be encouraged in a direction of retreat, which it will naturally seek if not provoked.

The bite of our small rattlers is rarely fatal, though it is unfailingly painful. Carry a snake bite kit and know how to use it before

Below: *The best steelheading starts at dawn, and ends when the sun strikes the water. It's the lucky angler who gets to trudge through the sage toward camp with a fly-caught hatchery fish bumping gently against his wadered legs.* JIM SCHOLLMEYER

you get into a situation where you must. Your brains are apt to be scattered if you ever need it. Current medical advice is to get to a doctor as quickly as you can. On the Deschutes that means get to your car if it's near, hop in your boat if you're floating, flag a jet boat or drift boat if you are hiking. Your trip is over. Don't exert yourself; it spreads the poison faster.

You should always expect to see rattlesnakes on the Deschutes. In truth, on an average weekend on the river, I will not see a snake. They are not that common; their hours and travels do not that often overlap ours. When you do see one, or hear it buzz, freeze, then figure the best way to exit in the opposite direction. The snake will most often politely do the same.

One October, on a warm afternoon, a few of us found a rattlesnake stretched across a dusty road. We wanted pictures, so we surrounded it. The snake tried to crawl out of the danger zone, but we shuffled our feet and blocked its path. It merely tried a different direction.

A rattlesnake in a photo looks harmless unless it's coiled and appears ready to strike. We tried to get this one to coil. It wouldn't. We waved a stick over its head. It drew its head back. We poked at it. It still wouldn't coil, or even quiver its rattles. Finally we gave up and let it go wherever it wanted. It crawled slowly up a bank above the road, still the disdainful gentleman.

Jim Schollmeyer watched it go up the bank. "I've always wanted to touch a rattlesnake," he said sort of wistfully.

"You're crazy," I told him.

"I know guys that catch them," he said.

"They're crazy, too."

The snake was stretched out, purposeful in its task of getting up that hill towing all of its dignity. Its head and its tail seemed far apart, disconnected. Jim kneeled against the bank below the snake, put his hand out slowly, brushed the snake. It kept going.

Jim looked at his hand, as if it were magic. "Now I can tell Debbie and Shawn that I touched a rattlesnake," he said.

"They'll never believe you," I told him.

I kneeled and touched it, too.

Above: *Only the edges of the broad Deschutes ever get fished. Fishing from a boat is not allowed, and wading is restricted by depth and a forceful current, which add up to sincere danger if luck is pressed. The rest of the river is untouched: a source of constant renewal.*
JIM SCHOLLMEYER

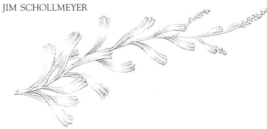

My rod was a light bamboo. The fly was an Elk Hair Caddis dry. I popped it to the water wherever an indentation in the shoreline might give a trout a place to avoid the swift current. A couple of trout came to the fly. I fought them short, bullying them to keep them off to the side, out of the main flow of the big river. One trout was small, around 10 inches long and lean for the Deschutes, though it would not have been lean on most rivers. The other was a nice fish, 16 inches long and heavy in the hand when I brought it in and released it.

Fishing was fine.

I stopped fishing after the second fish, to dry the Elk Hair on a handkerchief and dress it with dry fly dope. I blew on it to fluff its feathers and furs. It looked cocky, just as it had when removed from the tying vise. I rock-hopped 20 feet upstream along the edge of the river, out of the water, watching for snakes and poison oak. I spotted an indentation in the lee of a bunchgrass clump, and popped the fly to the water just where the grass stems wept to the water.

I saw a boil, the fly was gone off the surface, and the light rod bucked down toward the water all in the same instant. I could not hold this fish back from the main current. It was out 50 feet and then heading down, with the force of the river to propel it, before I could get the rod up and get a feel for how much strain my tippet might take. The fish felt big.

I held on while line spooled off. The backing knot twirled off the reel and ran up through the guides of the hooped rod. I watched the knot race out and chase the line downstream, sinking toward the water as it went. When the knot went into the water I decided it was time I went after the fish. It felt big enough to keep going if it wanted to. It felt too big to force back upstream if I ever got it stopped.

I rock-hopped down the way I had earlier rock-hopped up, this time without watching for snakes and poison oak. It was harder to maneuver while trying to hold onto the rod, watch where the fish went, and watch where my feet went all at the same time. At first I did not manage to gain any line; the fish swam faster than I could hop after it. When most of the backing was gone off the reel, and losing the fish began to seem likely, the trout suddenly put on its brakes, turned in toward the bank, and held there sullenly. I was able to gain some line then, adding the effort of reeling to all of my other duties as I tried to close in on the fish. I lost my balance once, but got it back just before I toppled toward the water.

I felt a sense of relief when the backing knot came back up out of the water, approached the rod tip, slid down the guides, and twirled back onto the reel. I lost the sense of relief when I saw why the fish held so sullenly. The leader was fouled over a limb that lay half submerged along the bank. Until

Above: *Arrow-leafed balsamroot is common in the sagelands alongside the river.* MARTY SHERMAN

Facing page: *A nice Deschutes rainbow: speckle-sided with a faint red stripe on the sides and blush cheeks, twelve to sixteen inches long, thick-bodied and full of fight. Even a small one can take you into your backing when hooked in a strong current. They should be held with the reverence shown here, admired a moment, then slipped gently back into the water. There are never enough of them.* BRIAN O'KEEFE

I got to it I could not tell if I fought the fish or the limb. When I got there it turned out to be both.

The fish was still on. I jiggled the rod and freed the leader from the limb. The trout, sensing my nearness, shot out into the heavy current again, turned down, made another run that exposed the backing knot but didn't take it past the rod tip.

Above: *Because the river is so rich, and its internal environments so varied, hatches are seldom so heavy that trout become unnervingly selective, tipping up selective noses at any but an exact imitation. But you will catch more fish if you have a general understanding of all that they eat. And you will certainly learn more about the river, and make some of its richness your own, if you nose through streamside grasses and bushes looking for tiny bits of brightness that have emerged from the river. Like the trout, you should take an interest in insects.* JIM SCHOLLMEYER

Right: *Too many caddis species to count live along the Deschutes River. They are the dominant hatch from June through August, and are especially abundant in bankside grasses and the sagebrush that grows near the water. They make awkward dancing flights out over the water, and often get onto it, and into trouble with trout.* JIM SCHOLLMEYER

I followed again, but this time was able to urge the fish into quiet water next to the bank and hold it there without any trouble. When I worked my way down to where the fish held in an eddy, it did not rush away from my nearness, but sulked deep. I moved to the edge of the quiet water, got below the trout, and backed it down to where I could reach it when it came up. Then I forced it to the surface.

Its dark form materialized out of the darker depths of the eddy, and it was about half the size I was sure it would be, not much longer than 15 inches. It would not weigh two pounds, though it was solid and would come awfully close. It wasn't as big as the largest of the two trout I had been able to bully earlier.

Some Deschutes redsides are extraordinarily hot. They fight far above their weight class. The currents of the river they live in are strong, and they know how to use them. It's not always the big ones that nearly spool you, though the big ones nearly always do some of their fighting in your backing, and force you to follow them downstream a ways.

Wild Deschutes trout are a redside strain of rainbow, adapted for thousands of years to their river. Its richness feeds them well; they are large. The stable flows of the springfed stream, compared to rivers subject to annual cycles of flood and drought, give the trout several extra weeks to feed every year. They are heavy for their length. The river's pushy current excercises the trout even as they go about their daily chores. They are strong. All Deschutes trout fight at least a bit above their weight class.

When the river was first fished, in the years around the turn of the century, it was full of these wild redsides. Settlers didn't have lots of leisure time; fishing pressure was next to nil. Access to the river was poor; it could be reached only at river crossings, at a few points in the canyon. Most of the water was sanctuary for its fish.

The coming of the railroad, in 1910, opened the lower river to fishing, though by today's standards pressure even then must have been relatively light. Chet Luelling, who was raised on the river and still lives on its banks, fished it not long after the coming of rails. In an article he wrote, "The residents of the whole central Oregon area could not have overfished the Deschutes before the arrival of the railroad."

Referring to the 1920s and early 1930s, Luelling wrote, "The Oregon Trunk Railway ran a night passenger train up the Deschutes canyon. The train left Portland in the afternoon, reaching Bend the next morning. It became a regular ritual for a group of business and professional men from Portland to charter a pullman coach for the Saturday afternoon departure from Portland. They would be in their berths as the train labored up the canyon at night. It was still dark when their coach was set on a siding at Mecca. The occupants would awaken to a day of fishing. Most of them took to drift boats and spent the day drifting to South Junction, where they took out of the river Sunday evening.

"The returning night train from Bend picked up their coach, which the fishermen boarded at South Junction. They were awakened in Portland Monday morning."

Pressure increased. Its effect was accelerated by the size of a typical catch. Early bag limits on the Deschutes were 35 fish, with a six inch minimum length. As access became easier through the 1920s and 1930s, such high limits took their toll. One can only regret, with what we know now, the numbers of small "trout" kept and killed that were undoubtedly downmigrating steelhead smolts that never did reach the ocean.

Limits were eventually reduced, but pressure was not, and trout populations continued to decline. In the late 1930s the Oregon Department of Wildlife took a far-sighted step. They closed the river to fishing from boats. This instantly created a source of sanctuary water for the trout. Populations of wild fish were again able to renew themselves. World War II reduced fishing pressure until the mid-1940s.

Shortly after the end of the war, the irrigation system on the upper river was completed. Crane Prairie Reservoir had already been in place for years. Wickiup was raised and filled to capacity by the end of the decade. Canals and ditches dewatered the

Left: *If Deschutes River trout could read a menu and order a meal, they might order up some caddis. Many caddis larvae are filter feeders; they build tiny gillnets on the bottom that balloon into the current. The worm-like larvae browse on whatever is captured in the net. Because plankton only grows in slow or still water, most rivers have little of it, and filter-feeding caddis are normally not numerous. But the dams on the Deschutes make lakes, plankton growth gets going, and the tiny plants and animals get swept downstream...and delivered to all those filter-feeding caddis larvae. That's why caddis sometimes come in clouds along the Deschutes.* JIM SCHOLLMEYER

Below: *A dance of caddis along the banks of the river. These flights usually start in late afternoon and increase as evening approaches. When the urge overwhelms them they fly out over the river and drop down to it, depositing the eggs for the next caddisfly generation. But many species don't stop at the surface; they dive into the water, swim with difficulty to the bottom, and affix their tiny egg masses directly to submerged sticks and stones. When finished they let go and attempt to regain the surface. Not many make it; most drown or get eaten by trout.* MARTY SHERMAN

Below: *Desert evening primrose sprinkle the summer sagelands with their occasional white blossoms.*
RENA LANGILLE

river at Bend and delivered most of the upper river to fields around Redmond and Madras. Irregular flows, high water temperatures, and siltation from the dams reduced about 100 miles of the upper river to a potential trout fishery. The whole answer to this problem would be a return to the way things were before the dams. A partial answer, badly needed now: guaranteed minimun flows through the entire portion of the upper river between the upstream irrigation dams and the downstream power dams, at a level that is livable to trout.

The 1950s and 1960s presented a new problem on the lower river, though it was thought to be a great benefit at the time, and not a problem at all. Hatcheries came to the river, and plants of catchables were used to augment wild populations without much thought about the genetics of the redsides.

The quantity of fish went up. As interbreeding between native redsides and hatchery fish increased, the quality of the population plummetted. Those gorgeous and brilliant red sides began to fade.

The river was in danger of becoming another put-and-take fishery in the 1970s. The Oregon Department of Fish and Wildlife took another long look forward, and instituted some new rules on the river. The first was to eliminate bait, restricting fishing to lures and flies only, with single barbless hooks. The creel limit was reduced to two fish per day over 12 inches in length.

Above: *Nighthawk rests and absorbs the sun while perching on a fencepost. The "hawk" is misleading; they are actually insect-eating nightjars, belonging to the same family as the eastern whip-poor-will. Nighthawks fly most often at evening, towering into the air, then diving and pulling up swiftly; the passage of air over their wings makes a sudden buzzing sound. If it happens right over your head it can startle you out of your shoes!* WORTH MATHEWSON

Perhaps most important, planting was curtailed. After a few more years of stocking in the most heavily fished parts of the river, it became evident that with the new regulations the wild population would do a fine job of stocking the river itself, without any added help. Planted trout, with their polluted genes, were no longer inserted into the river. The result was a gradual return to a better population balance between small and large fish, and the return of the native redsides as their better genetics reasserted themselves.

A secondary result of the new regulations, not so favorable, was a decade of high-grading: as people constantly kept their two legal fish over 12 inches, the numbers of large fish, 17 inches and over, declined. It became disappointingly rare to catch a trophy trout in the early 1980s.

In 1983, at the urging of Oregon Trout Executive Director Bill Bakke, the Department of Fish and Wildlife made another brilliant decision: they instituted a slot limit, allowing the killing of two trout between 10 and 13 inches. This let anglers keep enough trout for the frying pan, while ensuring that once a trout reached a certain size it would be able to keep growing to good size.

The result, just a few years later, is a river with its population of large, wild fish restored and still growing. It would be an unusual weekend trip now when my friends and I did not take two or three trout over 17 inches long. Some of the 20-inch-plus trout of yesteryear are starting to rise to flies again.

The Deschutes renewed itself so quickly, with the helpful regulations, because of its richness. Aquatic insect life is abundant. The river is famous for its late May and early June salmonfly hatch. The nymphs of these are black and large, up to two inches long. They are peaceful herbivores, browsing on algae and underwater vegetation. Salmonfly nymphs have been called the buffalo of streams; the Deschutes has herds of them that turn the bottom dark in places during their annual migration toward shore to emerge into the winged adult stage.

Salmonfly adults are just as large as the nymphs, and just as peaceful. They clamber in streamside grasses and willows, hanging over the water like fat berries. They are awkward, often falling to the water. Trout are glad to pluck them. Fishing their imitations produces some of the most exciting moments of the angler's year on the Deschutes River.

I once cast a Langtry Special up under a willow tree that hung close over the water. It wasn't easy to get the fly back into such a tight place; salmonfly imitations are so big and so brushed with hackle that they cast a bit like goosedown pillows. A redside boiled up to the fly. I yanked the fly out of there before the trout had a chance to hook itself.

I cursed at myself and cast again. The trout came again the instant the fly landed, and I jerked it away again the instant the fish tried to hit it.

I forced myself to gaze across the river,

Right: *Clouds, rain, and rainbows are not the average weather along the Deschutes. But an afternoon buildup of thunderheads and a subsequent blast of wind and rain, lightning and thunder are not rare in midsummer. One should go prepared for them whether hiking, fishing, boating, or camping.* JOHN HAZEL

made my eyes climb the cliffed canyon and gander around for a while, until I thought I was calm. Then I cast again and came unraveled. The trout detonated on the fly, I rared back to set the hook, and the leader snapped like a snippet of sewing thread. That leader was six-pound test; it should have

Below: *An early mist rises off the river, silhouetting a drift boat idled on the bank.* JIM SCHOLLMEYER

allowed me to land the willow tree that hung above the trout that now owned my fly.

Stoneflies are steaks, to the trout, but caddisflies are the most common groceries on the Deschutes River. Caddis larvae clamber among bottom stones, some of them feeding tranquilly on vegetation, others hunting down to death smaller aquatic insects. When caddis hatch they come off in clouds. I sat in camp one evening as the setting sun took a last

Above: *Natural salmonfly nymphs and flies that match them. These giant insects move toward shore in mass migrations every year in late May and early June. They are big and black and herbaceous; they have been called "buffalo of the stream." The nymphs crawl out of the water, usually at evening or after dark, and the winged adults emerge from a split in the nymphal skin. You can find these cast skins by dozens during the hatch, often in clusters on streamside stones that for some mysterious reason the salmonflies seem to prefer over other stones that look exactly like them, but are barren of cast shucks.* BRIAN O'KEEFE

backward glance at the river, through a notch in the canyon rim. Its low-slanted rays ignited something strange that hung like a halo around the top of a juniper tree not far from the river.

I picked up binoculars and tried to figure out what it was. Nothing became clear, so I stalked the tree. I was nearly at its base, still using the glasses, before I was close enough to see that the halo was a storm of caddis rushing in a circle around the top of the tree. I backed away from the river, stood atop the old railroad embankment, and looked out over

An early mist rises off the river, silhouetting a drift boat idled on the bank.

the sage flat between me and the river. The sun slanted across the flat. Almost every tree and every sagebush had its halo of madly circling caddis. Later they would fly to the river and drop down to it to lay their eggs. Trout would notice. Trout would applaud.

Caddis adults, like the salmonflies, hang around all day in streamside grasses. Unlike the larger insects, they are not so clumsy that they constantly fall to the water. But there are so many of them that at least a few caddis make parades out over the surface, and get into trouble with trout. The hatch is almost constant from June through August. During that entire period a dry caddis dressing fished along the banks will draw strikes from trout. My favorite is a size 12 Elk Hair Caddis.

Mayflies hatch on the Deschutes, too. Though these insects tend to be small and scattered, a few river experts know when and where to expect them, and how to match them. They do very well by imitating the duns when trout actively feed on them. But the Deschutes is a boisterous river; unlike most other famous trout waters in the West, you do not often have to match hatches with gossamer gear and tiny flies in order to fool a few fish. You can almost always excite them into striking larger searching flies.

The Elk Hair Caddis is a fair imitation of several species that the trout see day after day, through several months of the season. This makes it an excellent searching fly, for fishing the banks. I spent a summer season teaching fly fishing on the Deschutes, out of a school in Maupin. Every evening I hiked a group of students out and sprinkled them in favorite places along a mile of excellent bank water. I

knew it was excellent. Before the first class, I made an afternoon exploration of the bank myself, with an Elk Hair Caddis, to make sure I would be putting the beginners in the right places, and to be sure they would find fish there.

I edged upstream in waders that afternoon, fighting the current, staying tight against the bank on my right hand side, threading my way along the narrow transition line between dry land and water too deep to wade. It was tough wading, but worth it. Sometimes I had to switch the rod to my left hand, and hold onto a drooping willow or a streamside bunchgrass clump with my right hand, to keep the current from whisking me away. It made casting tough, but I seldom had to cast more than 20 or 30 feet, anyway. I used an eight foot graphite rod, a dry line, a fairly

Left: *Mating golden stoneflies. They are almost as large as the salmonflies, and almost as abundant. The hatch is similar, but starts a few days later, often overlapping, so that when you nose through streamside grasses and alders you never know which species you will encounter. Both are beautiful, emerge in great numbers, and are important to trout.* JIM SCHOLLMEYER

Below: *A mass gathering of salmonflies and golden stones on the bark of a streamside alder. Sometimes in afternoon the air over a riffle seems to be just as crowded with the same insects. Because the stoneflies are so big — an inch and a half long — trout take a severe interest in the egg-laying procedure.* BRIAN O'KEEFE

55

Left: *A big creature and a satisfying mouthful for any trout, the Western Green Drake mayfly hatches on the Deschutes — you see an occasional specimen bombing over the boat in late June or July — but is primarily an insect of the brisk headwater tributaries. The Metolius has them in its rocky gorge water; Fall River has good hatches throughout its cold and clear length.*

DAVE HUGHES

while the nymph plunges to the stones and thumps along the bottom. If no fish takes, the fly is allowed to rise on a tight line downstream. Then it is shot-putted back upstream, allowed to plummet and bounce along again. Often the take occurs right under the rod tip, almost at the angler's feet, which gets a guy to dancing.

Sometimes this deep nymphing method produces a lot of takes on the Deschutes. I have seen Holy Rollers land four fish to every one I could entice to a dry fly.

Another effective nymphing method requires a slightly more elaborate setup. It is called "indicator" fishing, and also puts the fly on the bottom. But the nymph itself is small, and either lightly weighted, or not weighted at all. From one to four split shot are pinched to the leader about a foot above the fly. The number of shot depends on the depth of the water and the force of the current. The deeper and stronger the water, the more shot required to get the nymph to the bottom. A strike indicator is fixed at the junction between leader butt and fly line tip.

The indicator is anything small, buoyant, and bright. Most people use an orange steelhead Corkie, running the leader through the hole in its center, holding it in place by

stout leader the length of the rod, and a size 12 Elk Hair that I had to dry and dress every few minutes because fish kept eating it.

I do not normally try for numbers of fish, nor do I often count the number of fish I catch. But I was ruthless that day; I wanted to know what this stretch of river held before I sent students out to fish it. In four hours I released 50 trout up to 16 inches long. Then the wind came up and pushed me off the river.

Dry fly fishing is my favorite way to fish the Deschutes River. I like the light tackle it allows, and I like the boil or splash of a take that reaches its conclusion up on the surface of the water, where I can see it happen. But the dry fly is not always the most effective way to fish the Deschutes, if sheer numbers of trout are what you are after.

A group of fly fishermen from Portland fish the river a lot. I fondly call them the Holy Rollers. They fish with heavily-weighted nymphs, big black imitations of the herds of salmonfly nymphs that live down on the bottom. Such flies must be cast with long rods and heavy fly lines, size 7 or even 8. Casts are upstream, very short, and the rod is held high

jamming the end of a toothpick into it. The indicator setup is fished with upstream casts. The nymph is allowed to sink, then to tumble along the bottom toward you. At any hesitation in the indicator's progress downstream, raise the rod to set the hook. Most of the time it's the lead shot ticking the bottom, but often enough it's a trout interviewing the nymph.

Traditional wet flies are rarely used on the Deschutes River today, but a new kind of wet fly is quickly gaining a reputation as a killer on the river. These are "soft-hackled wet flies." They are alarmingly simple flies to tie: The body is wound of the working thread; a single turn of hare's mask dubbing and two turns of partridge hackle finish the fly. That's all there is to it.

Soft-hackles are as simple to fish as they are to tie. They work best in riffles and broken runs. All you've got to do is cast them across the current, let them wash their way around in a quarter circle until they are straight below you, take a step downstream, pick them up, cast them again, and let them fish that quarter circle for you, almost without supervision. It's the old wet fly man's method called "chuck and chance it." It works on the Deschutes. It takes a lot of trout for me.

Like any other river, the Deschutes shelters most of its trout in a small percentage of its water. Learning how to read the river will instantly increase your catch because it will put your fly over water where trout will see it, rather than empty water. There's an old saying that if you fish where they aren't, you aren't likely to catch them. It's true.

Where they are is in riffles, broken runs, along the banks, and in eddies.

Below: *It is easy to walk the banks without ever noticing them. The dark bold shapes hover among the rocks, and seldom reveal themselves, moving to the top only to intercept an insect floating on the surface. When one is spotted like this it is almost too late; it will drift out of sight the instant the angler starts down toward it. But such a trout doesn't have to be hooked to make a day worthwhile. Just seeing it, knowing the river holds trout like it and that there is a chance to* hook them, adds an element of excitement to fishing on the Deschutes. ...and then it tips up for an insect, its snout out of water, making only a tiny dimple so you would think it a tiny fish if you didn't know that the largest of them conserve the most energy while feeding. You wait for it to go back down, then you make your cast, and you hold your breath, waiting for the sip and subsequent detonation. RANDY STETZER

57

Riffles are shallow, with a swift current, and reflect cobbled bottoms. The surface is choppy, bouncing along until the water gets deep and the surface smooths out because it no longer reflects the bottom. That is where a riffle becomes a run.

Riffles are productive for several reasons. First, aquatic insects love to live there, and trout find a lot to eat. Second, cobbled bottoms have lots of rocks to break the current, so trout find plenty of places to hold without fighting the river. Third, the water is shallow, so trout can see dry flies on the surface, and don't have far to spear upward for them. Fourth, if you fish nymphs, it's easier to get them to the bottom in shallow water, and easier to get news about it when a trout takes your fly.

Riffles on the Deschutes River are broad, rocky, and immensely productive. Some riffles on the river hold hundreds of trout, though the water can be so difficult to wade that you will be able to reach and cast over just a tithe of them, which is why the river renews itself.

Broken runs are fairly smooth on the surface, but boils and standing waves denote boulders below. Sometimes the boulders protrude through the surface. All of them, visible or invisible, make perfect lies for holding and

Right: *Workings of an old water pump abandoned along the river downstream from Macks Canyon. It was once used to lift river water up to the railroad tracks, to refresh engines on the long grade upstream.*
JIM SCHOLLMEYER

Facing page: *To many fly fishermen, holding a big brown trout in hand, especially when it is taken on a dry, is the ultimate thrill in the sport of fly fishing.*
BRIAN O'KEEFE

Above: *Seethings of small and delicate craneflies gather on streamside rocks throughout the summer, mating and depositing their egg masses on half-submerged streamside stones. The area must be wetted* *for successful breeding; the fragile creatures are constantly battered by the lapping of wavelets. Many are swept away and drowned, or get eaten by waiting trout.* JOHN HAZEL

feeding trout. If the water is three to four feet deep, you can wade cautiously along, popping a dry fly above and below the boulders, and in the slicks that form between them. A nymph tumbled into the pillow of slow water upstream from a rock, or cast into the slack water behind it, will often coax a trout to dart out to nail it.

This seems a place to insert a warning about wading the Deschutes: its runs are the most difficult and dangerous to wade, though the riffles and even the bank water can trick you into a tumble. The river is powerful. Because of the dams upstream, and consequent siltation, the bottom is slick. Always wear felts on the soles of your wading shoes, or better yet, wear the new felts with tire studs stuck in them. Always carry a wading staff tied to your belt. I prefer the folding kind that fits in a holster on my wading belt. It is always there when I need it, never in the way when I don't. I would not fish the Deschutes without it.

If you get into trouble and can't get out of it, don't panic. The river is going to give you a ride, and get you all wet, but it isn't going to do much more. You and your waders have neutral buoyancy; dogpaddle to keep your head upstream, ride the current feet first, and work your way toward shallow water as you can. If you go under, get your feet down and push toward the surface when they strike bottom. The river is not so deep that you won't be able to pop up often enough to get your breath.

Deschutes River trout love to hug the banks, because so much food is there for them. Most bank fishing is dry fly fishing. The trout wait for something clumsy to be delivered from the grasses or willows. They quiver on cocked fins, ready to flash to the surface. They are accustomed to making quick decisions, which is why searching flies, rather than exact imitations of some prevailing insect, work just fine most of the time.

A couple of approaches to fishing work well along the banks. The first is to wear waders, and move slowly upstream along the thin transition line between shore and the deeper outer current. It makes difficult going, but can be very productive. It's how I did it on that 50-fish afternoon. You've got to be very careful, especially where the water shelves off quickly, and where the boulders on the bank are large. Sometimes you will want to leave the water, go around an obstacle on shore, and re-enter the stream above it.

At times you will have to pull yourself along, casting with one hand, grasping vegetation on the shore with the other. This works fine; it's the way I do a lot of my fishing on the river. It gets me into places that few other folks visit with flies. But be warned: don't ever grab without looking. You don't want to come up with a handful of poison oak leaves, and you don't want to grab something that grabs back.

Right: *Clean streambed stones are the only hope for any river. Bill Bakke, a noted conservationist and Executive Director of Oregon Trout, has said that silting is already in progress on the lower Deschutes, caused by the return of sullied irrigation water. He predicts that in two to three decades fishing will begin to deteriorate, if nothing is done, because spawning beds will become impacted.* RENA LANGILLE

The second way to fish banks is to walk them dry shod, in sturdy leather hiking boots. Fish the indentations in the shoreline or wherever you can poke a fly under drooping alders and shrubs. Stalk the water carefully; most of the people I see fishing this way spook fish out of an opening long before they make their first cast to it. They don't even know the trout have already fled. They don't have a remote chance to catch a fish.

Hit each piece of bank water with a few quick casts, then move on. If fish are there and ready to rise, they will most often take the fly on the first or second cast that covers them well. The less time you spend rooted to one spot, pitching the fly uselessly over the same water, the more likely you are to catch lots of fish in a day. You also get to cover lots of ground and see lots of water. It's part of the reward for fishing this way. You'll end up the

evening tired, and a long way from the car. But the hike back gives you time to reflect on the fish you've caught, the adventures you've had, and all of the things you've seen that you wouldn't have seen at home.

The Deschutes is a windy river, so windy that it can ruin your fishing at times. Wind is almost a constant on the flatlands above the river. The canyon twists the wind's tail, and speeds it up. Most of the time you can fish when the wind blows if your gear is stout enough. That is why most experienced fly fishermen use lines in the No. 5 and 6 weight class, rather than featherweights in the No. 3 and 4 class. Heavier lines continue to carry flies into the wind.

If the wind gets too strong, learn to use it. Keep it at your back, and fish with it. Let it lift your fly and drop it to the water ahead of you. If it gets so strong that you can't control your casting, and wading gets uncomfortable because of all the buffeting, get off the river. There's plenty of other things to do. Go explore; do camp chores; read a book in the lee of your tent. If you're boating, run some river.

You can avoid the wind, most summer days, by fishing early and late in the day. Get up before the wind does. Fish until it begins to snort. Then quit; wait for the wind to blow itself out. Fish again at evening. Most of the time the wind lies down an hour or two before dark.

The Deschutes can seem a difficult river at first, especially to a person who hasn't had a lot of experience fly casting. It can be tough to

Left: *Teasel backlit by the sun.* RENA LANGILLE

extract that first trout from it, though after that it becomes magically easy. It is large, and sometimes hard to read, to find its fish. Wading is tricky if you don't own the right equipment: felts, or felts with studs, and a stout wading staff.

If you are not equipped to wade the river, stay out of it. Fish dry shod along its edges. Treat it as you would a small mountain stream: poke along and probe the shoreline, picking its pockets. It works. Trout are there, waiting impatiently for your flies.

But Deschutes River redsides don't look, and don't fight, like any of the eager little trout you'll catch from a small mountain stream.

Facing Page: *Some of the most popular and effective flies for Deschutes River trout include (top, left to right): Elk Hair Caddis, Deer Hair Caddis, Adams, Royal Wulff, Stimulator, Improved Sofa Pillow. Second Row: Kaufmann's Black Stone, Kaufmann's Golden Stone, Gold Ribbed Hare's Ear, Pheasant Tail, Zug Bug, Tied-Down Caddis. Bottom: March Brown Spider, Partridge and Orange, Partridge and Green. Dressings for these flies are all given in Appendix A.* ANDY CIER

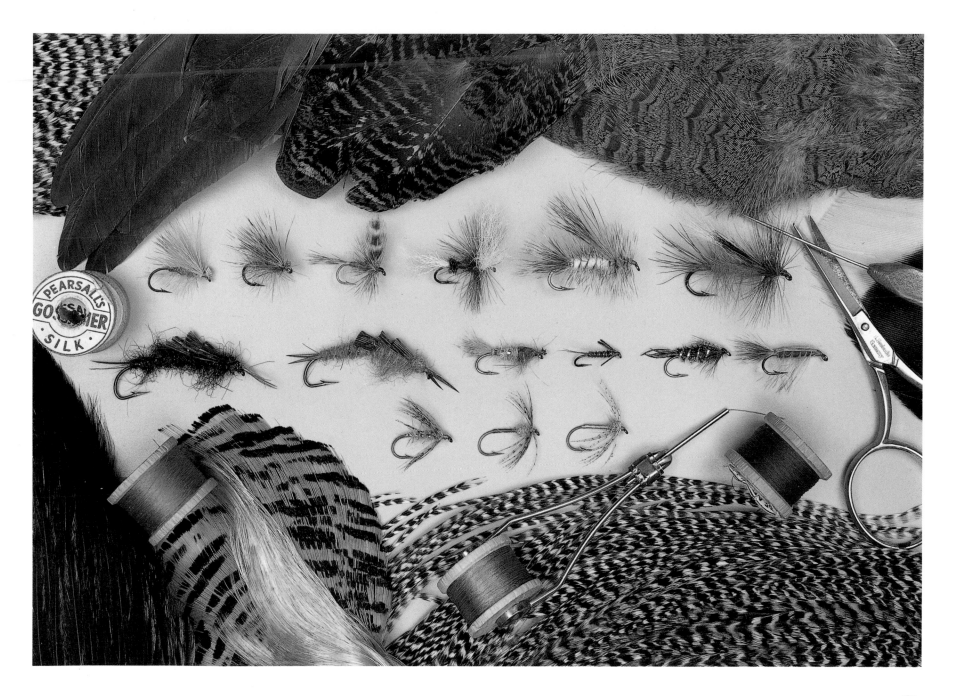

Steelhead Fishing

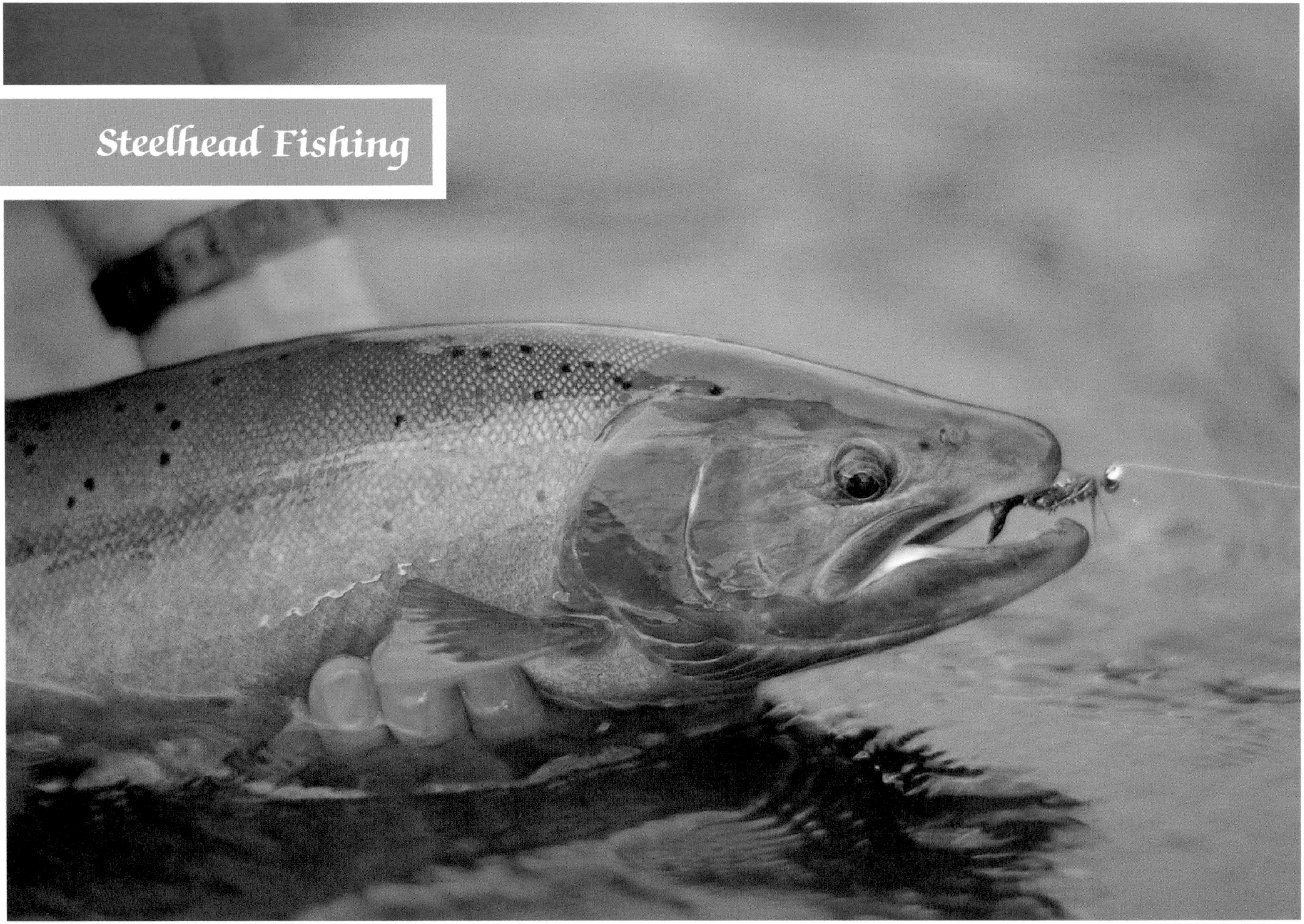

I turned the flashlight off. Mist rose off the run into the fall dawn. It looked like perfect water in the little light that struck it. The main force of the river swept around the outside of the bend, pushing up into standing white waves barely visible against the far bank. The water on the inside of the bend flattened out in a long and broad sweep three to six feet deep, with a moderate current that looked pushy, but not brutal. An uneven ripple on top of the water reflected a rough rock bottom beneath. Boils and slicks indicated the presence of an occasional large boulder.

There were lots of places down the length of the run where a summer steelhead might hold.

I heard a jet sled downriver, its irritating whine bouncing off the canyon walls, coming closer. Somebody was on the move already, making things urgent that shouldn't be. I zipped my flashlight into an inside pocket of my vest, and stepped into the run before I had time to assess all of its possibilities. I stripped line off the reel, began working it in forecasts and backcasts out over the run.

My first cast had just reached fishing distance when the sled appeared, a small blackness racing out of the larger blackness that was the bank curving away downstream. I let the fly drop to the water. The sleddist spot-ted me as my fly began its first teasing swing of the morning. He twirled the boat in an angry circle and pounded off over his own wake. I was on the water he wanted.

I'd camped next to it all night.

My casts were awkward and my wading clumsy for the first 15 minutes. But I soon settled down, worked the kinks out of my casting, and slid my feet the customary two or three steps between casts without stumbling. I was into the rhythm of fly fishing for summer steelhead: step and cast, step and cast. When everything is going exactly as it should, the rhythm becomes a pleasure of its own, removed from any possibility of fish.

I worked the run for an hour, wading its length, covering all of the water I could reach with the searching swing of a size 4 Green Butt Skunk. As light grew I looked around. The basaltic canyon walls were alternately dark and light where soil had formed and tan grass had grown between the black lava flows. A movement caught my eye on the hillsides. The little binoculars that I always carry picked out the silhouettes of a couple of deer, a doe and fawn, browsing in a high patch of grass.

A couple more sleds went by, rushing upstream. One slowed down, but picked up speed again and kept its course when its driver saw me.

I backed out of the run and hiked the quarter mile back upstream to where I had started fishing in the half light. I looked around then, and could easily see that I had entered the run too far down, about a hundred feet from the corner, below the precise spot where the main current broke over toward the outside and left the shelf of the shallow flat forming on the inside. The corner is often the best water down the entire length of a steelhead run. I moved up and waded out, staking my claim to the water again. Then I changed from the dark Skunk pattern to a brighter Fall Favorite in the same size.

Above: *The author found this bouquet of wildflowers in a camp on the lower river, after a boating party had just pulled out.* DAVE HUGHES

Facing page: *It's a big fish, and it started as a tiny egg here on this river, just upstream, buried deep in the gravel. It wriggled upward, fed dashingly in the river for two years then went out and gathered two or three years worth of mystery in the ocean before returning with it to get stunned by your fly and stopped on its way back to where it began, to begin it again. It lies exhausted in your hands, knowing nothing but its purpose, not even fear.* BRIAN O'KEEFE

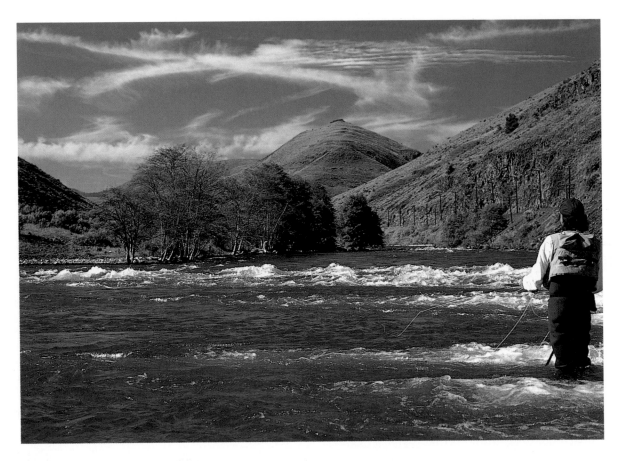

Above: *Careful wading can put you into position to fish the first calm water just below a tossed rapid: one of the best places to drift a dry or sink a nymph in search for hungry trout.* RANDY STETZER

I worked line out, making the first casts short, just at the edge of the fast current, letting the fly swing in an arc across the calmer water to the inside of it. When it hung straight downstream I picked it up, cast again a little longer. When the line was out to fishing length, 55 feet or so, I began working down the run again, cast and step, cast and step. I had almost reached the place where I had entered the run at daylight, was almost fishing the same water I had fished before, when I felt a great thud.

I raised the rod, let go of my slack, and instinctively shouted, "Ho!"

Nobody was around to hear.

The fish felt the hook, made a quick surge downstream, came up and flapped a couple of times in the air. It tumbled into the water, ran downstream again, came up again, then dug into the main force of the current with its tail and took off. The backing knot flew off the reel, out the guides, and dove for the water in a rush. I held the rod high and backed out of the run in a shower of spray. As soon as I hit dry ground I took off at a clumsy, wadered trot after the fish.

By the time the fish turned and held against the current I was winded from running in waders. I dropped out of my trot, but kept walking, cranking the reel handle madly to regain some line as I moved toward the fish. A sled came by, heading downstream. It slowed to watch me play the fish, then lifted up into planing position and whisked away.

When I got even with the resting fish, it punched upstream, jumped again, then ran back to where I had hooked it. I followed slowly this time, content to have the fish above me. It fought both the current and the rod for a time, then began backing down, surrendering position for the first time.

But the beginnings of surrender and the endings of it are a long time apart when the fish on the line is a Deschutes River summer steelhead. The fish had lots of energy left when we came together again. It used the current to run downstream past me, but this time it held to the inside of the main current, and without the river's force the run was weaker, shorter. I followed, but kept the rod tipped to the side, throwing the fish off balance, forcing it closer to the bank as I moved down toward it.

When we came together again the fish was tired. It swam in diminishing circles while

I kept rod pressure on it. Twice I tested it by lifting its head out of water, but both times it got its head under again and made short runs.

Finally I felt that the fish was ready to land. I forced its head to the surface, hooped the rod into a deep bow, and led the fish across my left hand. I lifted the hand just enough to strand the fish out of water. It flopped weakly, but could not get a grip on anything with its tail. It lay still. I kneeled and raised it enough to guess its weight at around seven or eight pounds, a nice Deschutes fish but not more than a pound or two above average size. Its caudal fin and tail had sharp, square corners: it was wild.

I twisted the fly out of the steelhead's mouth, lowered the fish to the water, held it a moment. It remained still, its jaws opening and closing. With a sudden and powerful thrust of its tail, it tossed water on me and was gone.

I stood up, wiped water from my face with a handkerchief, then moved back to the bank and sat on a rounded rock. A sled came by, didn't see me, moved in. Two men got out, stepped into the run, began to fish. When they were halfway down the run one of them saw me. He stopped fishing, confused by my presence, not knowing if he was poaching my water. I appreciated his concern. I swept an open palm in the downstream direction, offering him the water he was already fishing. He waved thanks and cast again. Far down toward the bottom of the run, where I had already fished, he hooked a steelhead and landed it.

His was bigger than mine.

Historically, summer steelhead ran and spawned in the main Deschutes all the way up to the first unpassable falls, in the canyon below Bend. They also spawned in the lower reaches of some of the tributaries, including the Metolius and Crooked Rivers. All of this upstream spawning and rearing habitat was cut off by Pelton Dam in 1958. Mitigation was

Below: *Almost every summer fires, usually started by railroad operations and campers along the river, race up the hills and leave sections of the landscape scorched and black. During construction of the railroad beds, one of which shows as the lowest layer above the river, crews rowed across the river at night and lit fires to race up into the opposing camp.* FRANK AMATO

Left: *At one time the main means of transportation in the area, and usually overworked, the horse now has most days off to nibble at pasture grasses alongside the river.* FRANK AMATO

made by installing a hatchery at Pelton. Now approximately half of the returning steelhead are factory fish.

Wild steelhead are far better takers, especially to flies. It might be their upbringing; before leaving the river for the ocean, they make their living eating insects. The instinct to strike might be retained. Whatever the reason, though half of the fish come from the hatchery, you will catch two to three wild fish for every one with a clipped fin, although their numbers are apparently equal.

Because of their willingness to take — which in the eyes of anglers make them a superior fish — wild steelhead were caught and killed more often. Their population needed protection. Starting in the 1970s regulations went into affect requiring the release of all wild steelhead. The bag limit on the river is now one hatchery steelhead.

Deschutes steelhead are not a large strain. They average five to six pounds, though of course in fishermens' terms this works out to seven and eight. There's nothing wrong with

that; they gain a pound or two in respect for the way they fight. Many of them weigh well over 10 pounds, without any added.

Steelhead from the Snake River, heading up toward the Clearwater in Idaho, nose into the Deschutes every year. These are big fish, and strong. They run 12 to 20 pounds. In October of 1946 Morley Griswold, ex-governor of Nevada, landed a state record 28-pound fish. It was a Snake River steelhead holding in the lower end of the Deschutes River.

The Deschutes River run begins to enter the river in late July, builds through August, peaks in September and October. Now that the river is open to fishing the entire year, steelheading stays good through November and into December, if you don't mind fishing with frigid hands. The fish are hottest, and fight best, when they enter the river, the fire in their fight cooling a bit with each passing month.

As time goes on the fish move up. They are found mostly in the lower miles of the river in late July and August, with the best fishing in the unroaded 23 miles between Mack's Canyon and the mouth of the river. By September they are spread through the roaded mileage from Macks Canyon upstream to, and even above, the town of Maupin. In October they are scattered in the entire 100 miles of the lower river below Pelton Dam. It is possible to combine trout fishing with steelhead fishing in fall, though there is a strong superstition against that.

I fished for steelhead once with publisher Frank Amato, and mentioned that I might fish a dry fly for trout while the sun was at the top of its arc. "Don't think trout!" Frank said. "You'll bring us bad luck."

When steelhead reach the mileage between Warm Springs and Trout Creek, I like to take a chance with superstition and fish for steelhead at dawn, nap a bit, fish the mid-day hours for trout, then fish for steelhead again at dusk. Without the nap it makes a long day.

Steelhead on the Deschutes tend to move upriver in indistinct waves. Every year their timing is slightly different. It's ideal if you have the ability to move when you are on the river, to find the fish. I drifted the river with the fellows from Wilderness Water Ways, in Corvallis, one year. It was a guided trip, and I was along to write a story about it. The first day the clients didn't touch a fish. Outfitters Jim Johnson and Dave Jobe butted heads in a conference, and decided to get some miles behind the drift boats the second day. The river whisked us along for hours, we got downstream 20 miles, and at dusk guide Steve Penner and I both took fish: eight pounders, of course, since you weren't there to weigh them.

The crew made a big camp that night. The next morning clients began getting plucks, and finally solid takes. Because of the long move, we had found the fish.

Reading steelhead water is the key to catching fish. They don't hang out in the kind of water occupied by trout, though there is a certain overlap. Steelhead prefer long reaches with even flow and modest depth. The cur-

rent must be pushy, but not so strong you can't wade it. Some runs look good but lack sufficient current to please the fish. It takes a little experience to be able to distinguish between them. Veterans on the river take a glance at a run and call it promising or label it "frog water," too slow to be worth fishing, depending on its currents.

The bottom must be cobbled, always with some rocks of basketball and bigger size to break the current along the bottom, which is where steelhead hold. Since they hold there, and your flies usually swing above them, not far from the surface, the water should be three to six feet deep so they are willing to punch up to take.

Steelhead hold well in ideal runs, but they also hold in chopped riffles, sometimes where you would expect to find trout. I have a story that I like to tell on Rick Hafele, the scientist and noted author who co-authored *Western Hatches* and was the talent in the video *Anatomy of a Trout Stream*. Rick fished a broad riffle for redsides, and caught several feisty 16 inchers. Knowing that I was just upstream, and that I wanted pictures, he reeled in, walked all the way up to get me, and led me back down to his riffle. Rick waded out ahead of me, with the intention of hooking another of those hard-fighting trout so I could take some photos.

I followed him, but in order to idle the time until a fish took, I tied on a weighted salmonfly nymph, and fished it with short casts in the shallow water to the inside of the riffle, where I didn't even expect a trout. The water was only a foot and a half deep, and not exactly galloping along. I made a few 20 foot

casts, kept an eye on Rick, and kept my camera ready.

Above: *You can fish for years, never take one, and though you see them rolling, or in somebody else's ownership, they become almost myths to you. Then there is that one cast out of all the hundreds, sometimes the thousands, and suddenly the fish is there and on and fighting hard and it's not quite understandable until the fish is worn out and at your feet. You lift it to hold it gently, making it yours for an instant before releasing it to become the river's again, to become the river itself again. Even then, after the fish is gone, you watch where it went and still don't understand it all.*
FRANK AMATO

69

Below: *An import from China, the ringneck pheasant carries an abundance of feathers that delight the fly tier.* MARGARET THOMPSON MATHEWSON

My nymph got caught up in the riffle. I assumed I had hooked the bottom because the water was so slow and the nymph was so heavy. I yanked to dislodge it. It yanked back. The fish bolted, shot out past Rick. I shouted and he turned to see my line flying past him.

"That's one of those 16 inchers," he said. "That's just the way they fought!"

At that instant the fish came out and tumbled awkwardly through the air above the riffle, right in front of Rick. It was one of the true eight pounders; it took a long time to subdue it with my light trout rod.

Tackle for steelhead obviously needs to be somewhat stouter than tackle for trout. Rods should be 9 to 9-1/2 feet long. The inherent lightness and power of graphite makes it a logical choice over bamboo or fiberglass. The rod should handle a weight-forward line in No. 6 or 7 weight, though some people prefer a heavier No. 8 or 9 to fight the wind that whistles up and down the canyon.

Reels aren't much of a factor in trout fishing; most anything that will hold the line will do. It's not true for steelhead: the reel should be strong, have an adjustable and dependable drag, and have space for lots of backing behind the line — 200 yards of woven 20-pound test is not too much. You shouldn't cast over steelhead with much less than 100 yards, or you risk losing your whole line in the downstream direction.

Leaders for steelhead must turn over with fairly large flies, and must hold up against fairly heavy fish. The length of the leader should be the length of the rod, at most a foot or two longer. It should be tapered to transfer the energy of the cast down the line and all the way to the fly. The tippet should be a couple of feet long, and should vary from 15-pound test down to six-pound test. When the water is clear, and you want to fish when the sun is shining on it, then you might go down to four pound test, but do so with a high sense of adventure and low expectations of landing a strong fish if you hook one.

Flies for steelhead must please the fisherman more than they must please the fish. Steelhead are prompted to hit a fly by memory or anger, and do not feed selectively, as trout often do. The primary concern with steelhead flies is confidence. If you cast a fly you like, one you have caught fish with, even one that you have heard others have caught fish with, then you will be confident that if a fish sees it, the fish will strike it.

The Green Butt Skunk seems to be the favorite dressing on the river, with the Freight Train and Macks Canyon also taking an outsized share of fish. Anybody fishing with one of these patterns should have lots of faith in it, even if he has never had a twitch from a steelhead before. They are large, sunk flies, designed to be fished just beneath the surface. A few people have learned how to coax steelhead up to skated dry flies, but most fish their flies on teasing swings a few inches deep.

Frank Amato, who fishes the river as much as anybody and more than most, describes the proper technique for summer steelheading in simple terms: "Wade deep, cast long, move fast." The deeper you wade, the farther you cast, and the faster you step and cast through a run, the more water your fly covers, and the better chance that a steelhead will see it and wallop it.

I told Frank once that in my experience most steelhead hit within 40 or 50 feet of the bank. If I'm wading 20 feet out, that means I could cast short and still take most of them. He agreed; that's where they hit. "But," he asked me, "have you ever thought about how many of them see your fly farther out, and follow it in before taking it?" He's right, of course. Cast as long a line as you can handle comfortably, and you'll have a chance at the far fish as well as the near ones. But if you can't cast very far, you'll still have lots of chances at fish.

The deeper you wade, the more water you cover. It extends the cast. There are, however, times when I violate the rule to wade deep. If I think a fish might be holding in close, as happened the day I fished the trout riffle with Rick Hafele, I'll go through the run once while wading no deeper than my knees. This trip through covers the inside water. Then I'll go through a second time, wading deep, casting farther out.

Moving fast makes sense because steelhead lie sprinkled down a run. If you stand in one spot, casting repeatedly to the same water, they will never see your fly unless they happen to be right below where you stand. Sometimes they are on the move, and you can root yourself and still take an occasional passing fish. But it's far better to develop the rhythm — step and cast — and take your fly to the fish. Make your cast and fish it out. Take a couple of long steps. Cast again. Fish it out and step again. It gets to be a pleasure; a strike will come as a surprise, jarring you out of some reverie.

Setting up the swing of the fly is not difficult if you remember that you want to show the fly to the fish swimming briskly across the current. The fly should not creep; nor should it race. It should not go so fast that it breaks up through the surface, though some people intentionally fish "waking" flies.

In order to install the proper speed into the swing, you should angle the cast anywhere from almost straight across the current to 60 degrees downstream. The slower the current, the farther upstream you cast, giving the water more line to push against, speeding the fly up. If the current is fast, cast farther downstream, reducing the angle of the line

Right: *The moon hangs over the river in a red sky. Sunsets in the Deschutes country are often beautiful. Because the river is deep in its canyon, you've sometimes got to hike into the hills to get the best view of them. The author once was able to watch the sun go down twice in a single evening, simply by watching it set, then hiking higher up a hill to raise it again, and sitting to watch it set again.* SCOTT RIPLEY

Left: *The Deschutes is sprinkled with small islands, most with gravel bars built up around them. They are excellent hangouts for trout, and also give the boating angler that sense of separation from the rest of the world, the feeling that he has attained a place where he's not going to get bothered unless it's by an osprey, an otter, or a fish.* DAVE HUGHES

across the flow, giving it less to push against, which slows the swing of the fly.

Mending line also controls the speed of the fly. When a downstream belly forms in the line, in fast current, it whips the fly around behind it. By rolling the line up off the water and back to the water in the upstream direction, you remove the belly and slow the fly. Sometimes when fishing slow water, I intentionally mend a downstream belly into the line, letting the current pick it up, speeding the swing of the fly.

I watched Mike McLucas fish for steelhead once. It was a lesson in patience. Mike owns the Oasis Resort in Maupin, where many fishermen stay, and a necessary stop for a hamburger, or at least for a milkshake so thick that you'll have to eat it with a spoon.

Mike is a dean among guides on the Deschutes River. I followed him down a steelhead run once. That in itself is a valuable secret; if you fish with anybody who knows something you don't, always follow him through the run. Never get in front of him. You might get to the fish first if you do, but you'll also be demonstrating to an expert your entire litany of casting problems, besides missing out on the best schooling you could possibly get. Mike knew lots that I didn't. He made his casts quite a bit farther downstream than I would have in that water. His line cut across the current at a 45 degree angle where I cast almost straight across it. Then he mended once, and let the fly swing part of the way through its drift.

As the fly entered the last half of its drift, Mike began tossing tiny mends upstream, one after the other. This did a couple of things. First, it gave the fly a little bounce every few seconds, which Mike feels might interest the fish. Second, it slowed the drift, extending the time the fly was in the water. I asked him why he fished this way.

"I think steelhead are stupid critters," Mike answered. "The longer I can hang my fly in front of their noses, the more likely they are to hit it."

It makes infinite sense. I have since employed this mending tactic, and my number of solid takes has gone up. But you must always remember that what makes the fly do the right thing in one piece of water will make it do the wrong thing in another piece of water. There is no substitute for experience. As you begin to hook fish, your brain begins to recall what the fly was doing at the time of the strike. It won't necessarily be conscious. But, the next thing you know, you will begin to know when your fly is fishing right. You will feel it coaxing the fish.

Fighting a steelhead once you've hooked one is mostly a matter of hanging on to your rod, and keeping the fish in range so that you can deal with it. If the fish runs down with the current, which is what normally happens, you need to back out to shore and follow it if you can. If you can't, you need lots of backing on the reel. Try at all times to force the fish to

work against both the rod and the current. I have often seen a beginner strike a perfect balance, allowing a heavy fish to hang downstream on a tight line, so that the angler, pleasant fellow, essentially holds the fish suspended and does all the work while the fish takes a snooze. Then the fisherman wonders why the fight explodes just when he is getting worn out, and thinks the fish should be worn out, too.

At the instant of the strike, and all through the fight, be looking for a place where you can gracefully land the fish. A sloped bank with a sandy beach is best, but rare on the Deschutes. The best you will find, most of the time, is a shallow and rocky gravel bar. Play the fish toward it. Only when you can force its head up and hold it there should you try to lead it into shallow water. Don't lead it over rocks; it can injure itself internally. A fish that is to be released should be led to your hand, held in the water while the fly is removed, then restrained until it is strong enough to swim boldly away.

Because there is no way to tell ahead of time whether the fish is wild or hatchery, all steelhead should be handled as if they were wild.

If you want to lift a fish for a picture, cradle it gently with both hands, one under the belly, the other around the wrist of the tail. Lift it up, have your partner snap the shot, then get the fish on its way again as quickly as you can. If it's wild, the river needs its genetics.

Fly fishing is not the only way to take steelhead from the Deschutes. Regulations call for a single barbless hook. A spoon or

spinner cast with a spinning or baitcasting rod is extremely effective, though snobs such as myself would never be caught by their friends with anything but a fly rod in hand.

For years my friends and I have camped at the same spot on the Warm Springs to Trout Creek float, each October. There are always a few spin fishermen around, and they always seem to hook one or two steelhead directly across from camp, in deep, roily frog water.

Above: *Mike McLucas is dean of guides on the Deschutes, and owner of the Oasis Resort at Maupin. He is equally eloquent alongside his home river, or in boardrooms and in front of the legislature, testifying for the river and its wild fish.* JIM SCHOLLMEYER

Their success puzzled me for a long time; the water where they hook them looks terrbile to me. I would never fish it.

It finally occurred to me that the best water for spin fishing is not worth a cast to the fly fisherman. It's too deep to entice a fish up to a shallow fly, too deep or too fast to get a fly down, or has too many conflicting currents to fish a fly right. I had always thought that the best fly water was good because that's where all the fish held. I was wrong; they hold in lots of places. The best fly water is where the fly can best be shown to the fish, given the inherent restrictions of the method.

When I discovered that spin fishermen weren't in competition for my water, my nose lost a little of its tilt.

These days there are side-planers on the river. They wade banks so deep and fast that whenever I see one, I'm sure he's about to be

Above: *The fish ladders at Sherars Falls allow upstream passage of steelhead and Chinook salmon.* RENA LANGILLE

swept away. I don't know how they do it. I wouldn't have the courage to fish where they do. I don't want a fish that bad. Nor do I want a fish bad enough to stand in one spot and lower a planer down the current, letting it swing back and forth towing a plug behind it, letting it do my fishing for me. But they sure catch fish, and surprisingly, they release as many as I do. They release more, because they catch more.

It didn't take me long to figure out that this new breed of anglers wouldn't want to fish my kind of water, or the spin fishers' kind of water, any more than I would want to fish theirs. I suppose spin fishermen might be snots around side planers, considering themselves superior, but I haven't managed to overhear them in conversation yet.

Once I decided that none of us were in competition for the same water, I also decided that the rest of the fishermen didn't wear such black hats after all.

There is an angling etiquette, based on common courtesy. When it's violated, it will almost always be by somebody carrying the same kind of gear you do. That's because he's the one who wants to fish the same water you do.

Once, in the summer that I taught on the river, I had a line of clients strung along a steelhead run at polite intervals, fishing downstream eagerly and well, step and cast, step and cast. The good water went on for a quarter mile below my point man, and we had at least an hour of pleasant and rhythmic fishing ahead of us. I batted cleanup, at the back of the line.

A fisherman emerged from the trees, fly

rod in hand. He looked at my clients, looked at the water, then started to wade in at the front end of the line. Anybody who would step in front of a line of fishermen instead of the back would probably stand in one place once he got there. The rhythm that I had so carefully set up was about to decompose. I had to do something, but I didn't want to be as impolite as the fellow wading out of the woods.

Dale Dearborn, an excellent fisherman and pleasant companion, was the first fisherman going through the run. I recalled a voice that I had not used since my days as an Army officer. "Say Dale," I bellowed, "it looks like that fellow's going to wade in right in front of you!" Fishermen heard it two runs downstream.

The poor guy looked up, shrank a little, and disappeared back into the trees.

Facing page: *Some of the best summer steelhead flies for the Deschutes include the Steelhead Muddler (top), Fall Favorite, Macks Canyon, and Purple Peril (center, left to right), Freight Train (bottom on fleece patch), and the most popular of all, the Green Butt Skunk (bottom). Dressings for these are listed in Appendix B.* ANDY CIER

Whooping the Rapids

You don't know the Deschutes until you've felt it toss you around.

Jim Schollmeyer and I scouted Colorado Rapids carefully. It's rated at Class III, with tall standing waves and great hydraulics. It would be a Class IV if it weren't for a narrow passage that makes it possible to skirt the worst of it if you want to. Jim and I each rowed one-man hard boats, wee things for the river. We looked like a pair of ducklings dodging down the waves. Several times, upriver, we had passed floaters in bigger boats and they had shouted, "Hey, you plan to go through Colorado in 'those.'"

"Guess so," we quacked back. "We can't turn around and row upstream to where we started." Their doubts nagged at us, but Jim had taken Whitehorse, Boxcar, and a few other big rapids in his punt of a boat on an earlier trip. We had also both taken water in a couple of smaller rapids on this trip. Jim came out of Wreck Rapids with his gunwale almost level with the river. But I had bounced over the top of Wreck, and we weren't too worried about Colorado.

We arrived at it, parked our boats and hiked down to scout it. I looked at those tall hydraulics in the center of the run, calculated the dimunitive size of my boat, then ran a mental finger down an inventory of what was stowed in the boat, including several hundred dollars worth of cameras, fly rods, and camping gear.

I went through first, while Jim stood next to the rapids to take pictures. I drove as near as I dared to the edge of the standing waves, riding up their sides, perching on the edges of them, almost toppling off a few times. Gallons of water splashed over the bow and spilled in over the sides. The boat got heavy, loggy. I was close enough to the worst of the torn up water to hit it with the end of my oar. I could hear it growling at me, feel it clawing for me. If I got into it, it would casually flip me unless I somehow got awfully lucky. So I skirted the edge of it.

A fellow had sliced through the rapid earlier in a whitewater kayak, beached his boat below, and walked back up to watch the luck of others. He saw me flirt with the worst of Colorado and commented to Jim that I was a chicken. He was right. I was.

Jim bounced through the same way I did, while I took pictures. Then we both sat awhile, bailing our boats and watching other parties thread through. All were in rafts or kayaks; they wore swimming suits and life vests. It was obvious from watching them that they were ready to be tossed, were prepared for it, were probably hoping for it. All of them walloped straight down the center line, letting the hydraulics toss them around.

A standing wave lifted one raft and powered it right over, not flipping it, just slowly lifting one side of it and continuing to lift until the boat balanced on its edge. The couple inside leaped out, the boat toppled, and they swam through behind it. They were not laughing; I was close enough to see that their brows were furrowed with concern. One hundred yards downstream they caught up with the raft, tugged it to shore, poured water out of it, and then laughter spilled out of them. Suddenly the capsizing became fun.

I was jealous. I'd been there before. I knew their feelings were a combination of exhileration, fun, and fear.

Above: *Woolly bears that will one day become handsome butterflies are a common sight in the grasses at the water's edge.* DAVE HUGHES

Facing Page: *At the head of the rapids... The river takes on a different meaning to you after you've gotten on it, found your own ragged edge and felt it toss you around a bit.* JIM SCHOLLMEYER

77

Above: *There's more than one way to go through a rapid, and they're all good so long as you come out at the bottom safe. These folks did, but they weren't certain about it when Colorado flipped them, then spit them out. Their gear, which happened to be mountainous and is probably why the river got them, was all tied on securely. Minutes later they righted the raft, laughed at what had happened, and pushed off toward the next rapid.* DAVE HUGHES

It took a while for it to occur to me, there at Colorado Rapids, that the thrill of running rapids is in the feeling of being on the ragged edge. I had found the edge and ridden it out on a line just to the side of the highest hydraulics. All those other folks, in their larger boats or their kayaks designed for white water, had to get into the thick of it to find

the ragged edge. If they had gone where I went, Colorado would not have thrilled them. But it thrilled me. It doesn't mean the same thing if there is no chance you'll get into the river.

The ragged edge lies in a slightly different line for each size boat, for each individual, for each rapid. Many of the rougher rapids on the Deschutes — not nearly all of them — have lines where you can avoid even the ragged edge. It makes sense to do that if you drive an expensive hard boat, have your boat filled with valuable gear, or carry passengers you would not like to risk dunking.

There are different ways to use the river. Whooping the rapids, prepared to be tossed into them, prepared to enjoy it if you do go in, is one of the finest ways.

We fishermen, and I say "we" to be sure to include myself, with my slightly tilted fly fisherman's nose, tend to look at our own way of using the river as somehow the highest and best use. When I taught fly fishing for a summer on the river, the house in which we held the indoor part of our classes loomed right over the river. A rapid ran beneath the decks. I used to stand out there and watch all the folks tossing by in their rafts, brandishing paddles, flinging buckets of water at each other. They weren't fishing. How could they be so happy?

It took a long time to drill it into my head that they had as much fun running the river as I had when I fished. When I got my own little boat, and started finding my own ragged edge, I found out they were having more fun, at least at peak moments.

A lot of fishermen I talk to consider rafting and fishing to be conflicting uses on the Deschutes. In a sense they are. Rafters and fishermen are on the same river, sometimes on the same days, using the river for enjoyment in different ways. I have heard calls for limited entry on the river, to cut down traffic. But there are natural separations between boaters and fishermen, without regulation.

In the past fishermen used the river from April through October. Now it is open the entire year. Rafters only use the river in the hot mid-summer season, June through August. At that time of year the best hours for fishing are morning and evening, before the heat of the day starts to cook somebody in waders. The best hours for rafting are those that scorch, because that's when it feels best to get wet, and is least dangerous to fall in. So boaters and fishermen are separated by time of year or time of day.

The best water for fishing is in shallow riffles, bouldery runs, or tight along the banks. A rafter would have to go out of his way to leave the best whooping currents and interfere with a fisherman. Of course, there are those who do that, but common courtesy keeps most rafters out of most fishing water, and common sense keeps most fishermen out of rafting water. They are separated by distance, though at times it seems not by enough.

In the chapter on steelhead fishing, I mentioned different kinds of fishermen — fly, spin, and side planers — and noted that when one of them does something to interfere with your fishing, he usually carries the same kind of gear you do. It's the same problem here: fishermen drift the river, and would all like to drop in on the same riffles, the same runs.

Rafters paddling by are less likely to disturb us than we are to disturb each other.

Permit entry regulations would solve a problem that is already largely solved by natural separations: when and where different users want to be on the river. There is no question that the river is used a lot. Speaking for myself, I like the opportunity to be on the river whenever I want, rather than being told I can go to it only at certain times. With a permit entry system I would have to plan my trips to the Deschutes. Most of the time I bolt for the river when a break opens in my schedule, and I'm in need of renewal.

I try to separate myself from other users by being content to use the river where and when they don't. I would rather do it my way, and have the river open to me, than have somebody else separate me by denying me the use of the river.

It's likely that a lot of the uproar stems from a few large, and sometimes commercial, rafting parties that trample into campsites in

Below: *Even when small, Deschutes rainbows have the fat football shape that makes them such strong fighters when stung with a hook.* JIM SCHOLLMEYER

Above: *Trouble has just begun...*

unload their vans and trucks, pump up their rafts and kayaks, and load them groggily, annoyed by their hangovers. It's too bad those who seek solitude have to move out of the way, but it's better to stay away from the parties than it is to stay away from the river.

Different reaches of the river are best suited to different kinds of floating. Before even mentioning them, I'd like to insist you buy a book that details all of the river. It is called the *Handbook to the Deschutes River Canyon*, and was written by James M. Quinn, James W. Quinn, and James G. King in 1979. The book is astonishingly thorough; it lists and describes every rapid, major or minor, rates it for difficulty, and tells the best way

Below: *...now their possessions are floating past them...*

herds, set up stereos with amplifiers, and throw beer busts far into the night, dominating the entire vast canyon. Because camping areas are limited, it's hard to get away from such a party when it happens, especially if you are already in camp, set up, and they move in on you. It's too bad they do that, but I haven't read a regulation that installs respect for the rights of others in people who lack respect for themselves.

You can avoid these parties by staying away from large campgrounds on Friday and Saturday nights, June through August. Or camp far out at the edges of them, as far from boat launching areas as you can get. That's where they congregate. In the morning they

Above: *...and Oh Shit Rock in Whitehorse Rapids owns itself another boat. Everybody got out all right but a lot of gear was lost.* JIM JOHNSON

through it or around it. The warning signs of approaching difficulties are described so that you have a chance to put on the brakes, get out and scout a rapid, rather than turn a corner and find yourself delivered briskly into trouble before you are ready to risk it.

My copy of this book sits on the cooler top, always open in front of me, as I row downriver. The first trip down, I left it out in the open; it got rumpled from constant splashing. Now I keep it in a gallon zip lock bag, open to the page that describes the moment of the river I am in, pulling the book out

in placid places between rapids when I need to turn its pages.

The "Handbook" has lots of historical notes, and points out many interesting events that happened at places you pass as you drift. It is a guide that will keep you out of trouble, or tell you the best places to get into trouble if that's what you're after. But the book is much more than that: it's a book that puts you more closely in touch with the river.

The best canoe water, in fact the only canoe water unless you are an expert at whitewater canoeing, is in the upper river. There are several pleasant half day and full day runs between Wickiup Reservoir, far above Bend, and Lava Island, just a few miles above Bend. There are also several hazards in the upper river floats, including Pringle,

Benham, and Dillon falls. Going over any of these in a canoe is almost sure to drown you, which ends your trip early. Before you launch on the upper river, read the guide book carefully, and know what kind of water unwinds in front of you.

The Deschutes from Bend downstream to the lake behind Round Butte Dam, near Madras, is alternately too high and tortured to run or too dewatered and low to run, depending on irrigation needs. It is not recommended for floating.

The first drift boat or raft float on the lower river, below the power dams, takes you 10 miles from Warm Springs to Trout Creek. It is easy water, with no rapids above Class 1+, which in the rating system for rapids is hardly a rapid at all. This is a half-day floating, a long day if you're fishing, and a gentle introduction to the river. Trout fishing is excellent. You must have a fishing permit from the Warm Springs Indian Reservation if you want to fish the west side of the river.

The next float is from Trout Creek downstream to Dutchman's Flat, a few miles above Maupin. This is a 33 mile float, and takes two days, at least three if you plan to do much fishing. It includes Whitehorse Rapids, a two-mile Class IV, which some consider the most difficult rapid on the river. In the rating system a Class IV is described as "very dangerous." The railroad runs along this reach of the river; private roads come near it in places. For the most part it is only seen by boat or very determined hikers. Many miles of it go through the property of The Deschutes Club. They allow you to land and fish, but do not allow overnight camping on the property.

For the first 20 miles of this float the left side of the river is on Indian Reservation land, closed to all fishing.

Above: *Quizzical barn owl peers at the camera. Hunters of savanna and woodland, barn owls capture and devour rodents, and are at home, though not so often seen, in the sage lands along the Deschutes River. Those puzzling condensed bits of bones and fur sometimes found on rocks or beneath trees are not scat, as they appear, but pellets regurgitated by owls after they've digested the nutrients out of a mouse or ground squirrel.* JIM SCHOLLMEYER

The next float, from Dutchman's Flat down to the town of Maupin, is only four miles long, and is paralleled by gravel road. It brags about a condensation of fine and feisty rapids, including Class III Wapinitia and Class IV Boxcar, plus a lot of Class II+ rapids back to back. Boxcar is an abrupt beast, and trips a lot of boats. This is a short but energetic float, guaranteed to keep you busy and whooping. Some folks bang their cars up and down the road, in clouds of dust, eagerly repeating the short float three or four times in a day. Trout fishing is excellent in this area, the best of it along the banks. Anglers might feel abused by the number of rafters here on weekends when the weather is hot. But company comes with the territory: it's one of the best stretches to float.

The next float, from Maupin to Sherars Falls, is about eight miles long, and is the classic river run on the Deschutes. It takes half a day. Combined with the four miles of boisterous water above it, this will give you a full-day float on the part of the river with by far the most bounce to it. There are constant Class II and II+ rapids. In my own rating system, the first whoops get shouted out at about Class II. There's plenty to shout about here. Oak Springs Rapid is a Class IV, one of the most difficult on the river. Raft rental services in Maupin are set up to service this float with shuttles, and it is almost constant pandemonium on a hot summer weekend. Trout fishing is good along this section. The best fishing can be reached by hiking the road on the east bank or the railroad track on the west bank. If you try to float and fish it, you might feel surrounded.

Sherars Falls is a punctuation point at about the mid-point of the lower river. It cannot be run, though like most things that can't be done, it gets done by accident once in a while. Mark Angel, who makes part of his living salvaging boats that other people stick to the bottom of the river, even plunges through Sherars Falls once a year on purpose. Don't try it. Most people who fail to take out above the falls are lucky to wind up in the hospital. A friend of mine once caught one of the less lucky souls on his anchor rope.

Conestoga Rapids cuts through the same basaltic flow that forms Sherars Falls. It is only a few hundred yards downstream, and is a Class IV+, which means that it is rated at "more than very dangerous." Only experts should dare it. Most people start the next float at a sandy beach about a mile and a half below Sherars, near the entry of Elder Creek.

From Elder Creek to Beavertail is an eleven mile, half-day float, a full day if you fish. A few Class II rapids sprinkle this run at distant intervals, but most of the water is either flat or rumpled with mild Class I water. Only one Class III, Wreck Rapids, is enough to cause substantial whoops, and it can easily be lined around. Trout fishing is good in this reach, and you will also find some fine steelhead water. A gravel BLM road runs along the river on the east bank.

Facing page: *Dawn and mist and steelhead time.* GREG BLOCK

Left: *Benham Falls, on the upper Deschutes, was formed when the river, after centuries of being pent up, finally cut its way through a lava flow from Newberry Crater. The backed up water had spread out and allowed silt to settle. When the river broke through, forming the falls, the exposed lakebed upstream became a series of meadows that were once Indian hunting grounds, and are now farm and pastureland.* SCOTT RIPLEY

The next float is eight miles from Beavertail down to Macks Canyon. It is a placid drift, with only a couple of Class II rapids. It's a half-day float, a full day if you fish. Some good trout water exists here, but this is transitional water between the best trout water upstream and the best steelhead water, which is still downstream. The BLM road on the east bank ends at Macks Canyon, where you take out.

From Macks Canyon to the mouth of the river is a 23 mile float that could be done in a long day, though it is taken more leisurely if a camp is made mid-way. If you want to fish, leave yourself three days to cover some of the water, though you won't cover it all in that time. This is another unroaded stretch, with a hiking trail on the east bank and the railroad on the west side. The majority of water is relatively peaceful, but the float includes Colorado Rapids, a Class III, and Rattlesnake Rapids, a tricky Class IV with no easy way around it. This last reach of river is primarily steelhead water, though it also produces some fine trout fishing for those who are not superstitious, or those willing to take a chance on spoiling their luck for the larger fish.

Steelhead water draws the best-equipped anglers, and a lot of them count a jet sled as part of their equipment. The lower river sometimes seems to be seething with them; even folks who own them will confess that, with some signs of regret.

Jet sleds are a historic use on the lower river. They were running up and down it as early as the late 1950s and early 1960s, when there weren't many people around to be disturbed by them. Strangely, their use predates much drift boat traffic at the low end of the Deschutes River.

Most sledders are careful, and polite to exhaustion. I have seen them wait patiently at the bottom of a rapid, holding against the current, while a string of rafts and boats bounced through. I have also seen some sledders take chances, sliding up a rapid when a raft is already committed to the current, coming down without much control over its own direction.

Most sleds are operated safely. It is unfortunate that none of them can be operated quietly. The way their exhaust is vented makes them difficult to tone down. Somebody seeking solitude on the river cannot avoid the noise of a passing sled, short of climbing out of the canyon.

From the attitudes I see on the river, I suspect it is a matter of time before jet sleds are removed from it. I've never heard a drifter praise them. I've heard lots of sled owners decry the competitive aspect the sleds have introduced to steelhead fishing on the Deschutes. You've almost got to have one to get a good piece of water anymore, unless you can camp on it.

Different kinds of boats transfer the feel of the river to the boater in different ways. A kayak, hard or inflatable, puts you so close to it you almost become one with the current.

Inflatable rafts tend to smooth out the smaller bumps, so that you don't feel them. But rafts let you experience the hydraulics and standing waves in the biggest rapids, so that you get the feel of the water where others might gingerly step aside. They are the most stable craft, and filling them with water doesn't sink them. Rafts bounce off rocks, making minor problems out of what would be bad mistakes if you were running a wood or fiberglass drift boat.

A drift boat is rigid, and moves with every wave, rather than warping over them as a rubber raft does. You feel it all. The smaller the drift boat, the more you feel. But even a 16-foot drift boat will give you a thrilling ride through any rapid above a Class II. Wood or fiberglass drift boats do break, instead of bouncing off, if you hit a rock with a lot of force. Aluminum boats stick. If the force is strong enough they bend.

Jet sleds are so long and moving so fast that they flatten out rapids. If you go through a Class IV you won't know about it until you glance at your guide book later. I speak as a passenger here; I've been at the oars of the other kinds of boats, but I've never been at the wheel of a sled in a rapid. I could say I'd never been at the helm of one at all, but Frank Amato got me. He asked me to steer his boat briefly while he fiddled with some gear. I put my hat on backward, stood up to take the wheel, and Frank snapped me with a camera.

"For blackmail," he chuckled.

People drown on the Deschutes River every year. Sometimes, though rarely, it's a

Above: *Fence lizard takes the sun on a rock. This creature has an interesting concept of personal space. When first spotted it will squirt away, then stop abruptly perhaps ten feet from you and in plain sight, using its coloration as camouflage. Move up to it slowly and it will dash away again, then stop, but not so far away. Each time you approach it, the lizard will allow you to come a bit closer. If you can track it for thirty or forty feet it will finally let you move a hand up to gently touch it. This one has permitted something to get too close: it has lost its tail to a predator.* RENA LANGILLE

fisherman; those who fish tend to know the ways of rivers, and stay out of trouble. Most of the time it's an inexperienced rafter, on the river for the first time, unaware that there is anything but fun involved in whooping down it. Usually either alchohol or the lack of a life vest plays the fatal part.

Below: *Taking time to hike the banks is always worthwhile. Some of the miniature views, such as these Tiger Swallow-tail butterflies, form counterpoints to the beauty of the river and its canyon.* LEWIS ROSER

You cannot eliminate all the chances of getting hurt on the Deschutes. That is why there is fear at the head of the rapids: even if you do everything right, the river can still hurt you. The fear makes it a thrill to shoot down its rapids. You wouldn't want to eliminate it. But being safe doesn't rub out the thrill. It can increase it by daring you to get closer to the ragged edge.

Boating safety is relatively simple. Stay sober, at least when you are on the river. Always wear your life jacket. When you come to a major rapid, run the boat to shore above

it, get out and scout it. Choose your route through, deciding in advance how you will meet or avoid obstacles such as boulders, standing waves, and suck holes. The river will often direct you away from your planned route, once you are inside a rapid. It has its own thoughts about the direction of boats. But by having examined the rapid carefully, you will at least know how to get back on course, or how to ride out something you intended to avoid.

Sometimes you will have to ride out a rapid apart from your boat. Don't panic. Go out upstream from the boat if you can, and stay behind it. If you can't stay upstream from the boat, then move away from it to the side. Don't swim downstream ahead of a rudderless boat. One of the worst events is getting pinned to a boulder by all that great weight, with the force of the river behind it.

Ride out the rough water with your feet downstream, backpeddling with your hands to keep you head elevated and upstream. This allows you to see where you are going, and also allows you to fend off rocks with your feet instead of your head. Those who intend to take lots of chances should wear helmets.

If you're new to the river, it helps to run it with somebody who is familiar with it. But you don't have to do this. I intentionally ran the worst part of the river alone the first time I did it. It was a way of increasing my own fear at the head of the rapids, and it worked. I was very careful, had a great trip, and going it alone the first time has increased my appreciation of the river every time I've run it since.

You are required to have a boater's pass to float the river. The cost is negligible; the benefits great. Funds from the pass system have allowed the creation and maintenance of many campsites along the river.

The desert ecology of the Deschutes is fragile. Camping should be done on a "no trace" basis. Plan your trip so that you can take out the remainders of whatever you take in. Do all of your washing — dishes, your teeth, yourself — away from the river. Don't drink river water. Use a camp stove for cooking; open fires aren't permitted except in winter. If you use a campsite with no latrine, establish one at least 50 feet from the river, dig a hole six to eight inches deep, and cover it with dirt before you depart.

Leave no trace of your visit on the river of renewal. Let it leave its traces on you.

Right: *The wooden water tower at Harris Canyon is a landmark to steelheaders on the lower river. Some of the most interesting battles in the Railroad War took place up Harris Canyon, and along this reach of the river. Some of the best summer steelhead water lies in the same mileage, both upstream and down.*

JIM SCHOLLMEYER

JIM SCHOLLMEYER

Frank Amato

I fell deeply in love with the Deschutes River the first time I fished it, in early July of 1958, at Dry Creek on the Warm Springs Indian Reservation. To my teenage eyes, it was a powerful river in a stark, rugged canyon. The contrast of all that sparkling water, flowing between verdant green banks but deep in such an arid canyon, stirred in me a desire to know the river and its total ecosystem.

I walked and fished the river whenever I could that first summer, for it became quickly apparent that the river offered trout of a quality and size not found in the food-poor rivers on the western side of the Cascades. But the early allure of the Deschutes was much more than just that of its wild trout.

It was star-filled nights and the silvery reflection of the moon on the river's obsidion black surface, or the sweet evening perfume of the mock orange during the mid-June salmon fly hatch.

It was the sounds of morning doves and red-winged blackbirds and night hawks. It was the sight and sudden sound of a large trout taking a salmon fly, or the undulating movements of wild trout spawning in the shallows. The Deschutes was the pungent smell of sage and juniper after a summer thunderstorm, or

the daytime heat and harshness of the canyon's rock walls followed by the softness and coolness of evening. It was the unfolding of the universe as I lay on the ground in a sleeping bag, considering how insignificant we all are, and wondering if there might be another Deschutes River in the universe — or even beyond: a delicious hope.

I sweated along the hot banks while fishing. But it was sweet sweat, not the kind exuded by the immigrant Chinese and Italians hired around the turn of the century to break rock and drive steel rails up the canyon for 75 miles. Mine was a labor of love fueled on by the hope of discovery; theirs was based on survival.

Rivers provide many kinds of personal experiences for each of us. I have spent nearly a thousand days along the Deschutes over the years. The river is a much greater part of me than I am of the river. Rivers are great because they can never be one person's possession, like a coin. They belong to all of us. As their waters fill their banks, so also can they fill our souls with spiritual treasures: discovery, amazement, contentment, and yes, even fear. Sit back in a quiet place, close your eyes, and visualize your favorite Deschutes River experiences. Dwell on them for several minutes: your spiritual treasures need simply be recalled to be re-used.

The poetry of a river is movement. To move or be moved is satisfying, and is part of a vital and eternal link with the prime cause of movement. A grand, swift river is majestic in its movement, and touches the very essence of ourselves while also uniting like-minded companions in a type of baptism.

Below: *A gopher snake with ideas bigger than its mouth can encompass.* RENA LANGILLE

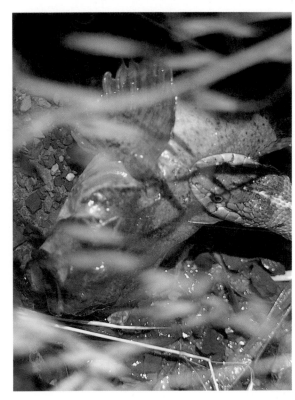

In spiritual terms, the Deschutes and other rivers are priceless for the personal renewal they offer to those who seek them out. In physical terms the Deschutes River benefits us in many other ways as well: we eat potatoes and chew mint flavored gum, irrigated by its waters; we read at night with light it provides; we eat its hatchery produced steelhead.

Irrigation and power dams interrupt the Deschutes in too many places already. Some people would like to see it dammed even

more. We, the protectors of rivers, act to save the magnificence and beauty of flowing waters for ourselves, and for following generations.

The original Indian inhabitants of the Oregon country used the river, as we do now, for both spiritual and physical reasons. Spring and fall salmon, as well as summer steelhead, were netted or speared for food, and for limited commerce, at waterfalls, wiers, or on shallow spawning beds. But their harvest was negligible, like a small stone thrown by a lad onto the river's surface. Things quickly changed when western man came into the Oregon country in the 1840s.

In my early trout fishing days, in the 1960s, I quickly realized that the river was being over-fished, and that if the state regulating agency did nothing then "quality" fishing would eventually disappear. The daily limit was 10 fish at that time, with a minimum length of six inches. Everybody kept what they caught; I did, too. But upon examining my motives for killing 10 fish a day, I discovered that what I really wanted most from the Deschutes was to be able to fish for its large, wild fish, its old fish, not six-to ten-inch fish, and not the hatchery fish that were being dumped into the river. At the end of a day, I didn't want my trout "dead."

Ten dead, wild trout ranging from 10 to 18 inches in length represented a total of about 35 years of river growth! I could catch and kill these fish in only a few hours, and thousands of fishermen were doing the same thing. The river's wild trout population was being ruined. By 1967, when I started *Salmon Trout Steelheader* magazine at the age of 24, I was an editor with a cause: to change the regulations on the Deschutes River. For the next four years, along with other like-minded individuals and fishing clubs, I lobbied the game commission.

In the fall of 1972 I sat in the audience and listened to the vote on our proposed conservation regulation for a 35-mile stretch of the best trout water on the Deschutes. It was a one-to-one tie when the Game Commission Chairman said: "I will probably regret this, but I vote in favor of the new regulation." It allowed only two fish over 12 inches to be killed, and restricted fishing to barbless hooks and artificial lures or flies.

That cornerstone 1972 decision has directed trout and steelhead management on the lower 100 miles of the Deschutes down to this day. It meant the river would be managed for wild fish, not for meat fishing. The concept of fish flesh to eat had given way to the spiritual effect of catch and release. It freed the wild trout and steelhead to propagate to their fullest extent, to grow and to die of old age. It also insured thousands of Oregonians, far into the future, a quality fishing experience on the Queen of Waters, and not empty waters.

In 1972 we fought another battle. The Bureau of Land Management wanted to open a road along the river for 50 miles, from the Warm Springs Bridge to Maupin. This would have destroyed the scenic, non-motorized aspect of half of the lower canyon. To gather support in opposition I published a point by point refutation of the plan in *Salmon Trout Steelheader*, with hopes of igniting overwhelming opposition to it. At a public hearing in Portland, then-Governor Tom McCall re-

ceived a standing ovation after he delivered his personal testimony against further development. BLM was stopped.

By the late 1970s boat and raft use was increasing dramatically on the lower 100 miles of river, from Warm Springs to the mouth. Governor Atiyeh appointed a Deschutes River Advisory Committee to study the river, hold public hearings, and suggest a plan of action. Covered were such problems as litter, fire, private boat use, commercial guides, and lack of law enforcement.

Out of this came the idea for a Deschutes River Boater's Pass, requiring boaters and guests to pay a nominal fee per day or season. The bill was headed for defeat in the legislature, holed up by the opposition in a committee. I was notified as a member of the advisory committee, and immediately asked the Association of Northwest Steelheaders for their support. They gave it and the bill was quickly passed.

That nominal fee has now raised more than one million dollars, all of it totally dedicated to the Deschutes and its environmental management. In addition, hundreds of thousands of boater use dollars have been used to acquire private lands along the river for public use. The Northwest Steelheaders made the difference, and can be proud of their accomplishment. Immediately after the bill was passed I received this note from a state parks official: "Around here we had dubbed H.B 3181 the *Phoenix Bill*; you helped it rise from the ashes and fly!"

In March of 1982, I received a strange request for a free ad, to be published in our magazine *Flyfishing*. Upon reading the ad re-

quest I was alarmed to learn that it proposed a private fishing club, the *Deschutes River Fishing Preserve*, with 200 members, each paying $7,500 for membership. The club would buy about 4,000 acres bordering the lower 12 miles of the river — from the mouth upsteam to Lockit — including both banks. Public access would be restricted.

This land had been for sale for quite some time. The asking price was less than two million dollars, but the state had not seen fit to buy it. The price was low enough that some wealthy person might snap it up, possibly even the Rajneesh, who was operating on the nearby John Day River at the time.

Above: *Special donors to the lower Deschutes land purchase have had their contributions to the river recorded on plaques alongside it.* FRANK AMATO

Facing page: *The Deschutes cannot constantly renew itself, or offer renewal to those who visit it, without help from those who love it.* JIM SCHOLLMEYER

Below: *Purchase of the land along the lower twelve miles of the river has assured that it will be open to everyone, forever.* JOHN HAZEL

I knew that the person proposing the private club purchase intended the ad request as a red herring to force the state into action. I immediately asked for a meeting with Governor Atiyeh, to demonstrate this threat to the Deschutes. I asked Chuck Voss, executive director of the Northwest Steelheaders at the time, and Douglas Robertson, who had proposed the club, to accompany me to the meeting.

I told Governor Atiyeh how important it was for the state to purchase this property for the benefit of all its citizens. Douglas Robertson played his cards by representing the private purchase. At the end of the meeting the governor said that he would talk to the State Parks people, and to the Fish and Wildlife Department, to see what could be done.

Within a few weeks the machinery had been put in place for a two-pronged fund raising effort, led by the Oregon Wildlife Heritage Foundation under the aggressive leadership of Alan Kelly. Public contributions poured in, as well as boater pass dollars, money from excise taxes on fishing and hunting equipment, and license money. The original $1.6 million purchase was made, and the momentum from that first successful drive led to the state purchasing other large parcels of property along the river as they became available.

Doug Robertson was the catalyst. He created the threat of private purchase, while all along wanting the state to buy the land, which it had declined to do for many years.

As the publisher of two sport fishing magazines, I can say that without a doubt letters make a difference — and sometimes have an immense impact. I acted immediately upon receiving Doug Robertson's letter. His inspiration was relayed to me, and then to Governor Atiyeh, and has resulted in almost $3 million of land purchases along the Deschutes River for the citizens of Oregon to enjoy.

Each river is unique. Those of us who love rivers have an obligation to protect them from damaging development, for a river is a public resource, not to be exploited by the few. And a river is not just the water it contains: it is also the riparian area, which offers a special kind of living space for many plants, birds, and animals, and secures the river bank against erosion, as well as providing shade, protection and food for the water and its fish.

The smallest gesture means a lot: watering a young tree in the heat of summer, picking up cigarette butts in a messy camp others have left, crushing and carrying out beer cans, picking up discarded fishing line. When we go to the river we should treat the river and its environment with the same respect we treat our own living room, for that is exactly what it is.

Appendix A - Trout Flies

DRY FLIES

Elk Hair Caddis
Hook: 1X fine dry fly, numbers 10-16.
Thread: Tan 6/0.
Rib: Gold wire, counterwound over body and hackle.
Body: Hare's ear fur.
Hackle: Ginger, palmered over body.
Wing: Tan elk hair.

Deer Hair Caddis
Hook: 1X fine dry fly, numbers 10-16.
Thread: Olive 6/0.
Body: Olive fur or synthetic.
Hackle: Blue dun, palmered over body.
Wing: Natural dun deer hair.

Adams
Hook: 1X fine dry fly numbers 12-16.
Thread: Black 6/0.
Wing: Grizzly hackle tips.
Tail: Grizzly and brown hackle, mixed.
Body: Muskrat fur.
Hackle: Grizzly and brown, mixed.

Royal Wulff
Hook: 1X fine dry fly numbers 10-14.
Thread: Black 6/0.
Wing: White calf tail, upright and divided.
Tail: Black moose body hair.
Body: Peacock herl/red floss/peacock herl.
Hackle: Coachman brown.

Stimulator
Hook: 3X long numbers 6-14.
Thread: Orange 6/0.
Tail: Deer body hair.
Rib: Grizzly hackle, palmered.
Abdomen: Yellow fur.
Wing: Deer body hair.
Hackle: Grizzly, palmered over thorax.
Thorax: Orange fur.

Improved Sofa Pillow
Hook: 3X long numbers 4-8.
Thread: Brown 6/0.
Tail: Orange dyed elk hair.
Rib: Brown hackle, palmered.
Body: Orange fur or synthetic.
Wing: Woodchuck tail.
Hackle: Brown.

NYMPHS.

Kaufmann's Black Stone
Hook: Extra long nymph, numbers 2-10.
Thread: Black 6/0.
Weight: 12-20 turns lead wire, flattened.
Tail: Black goose quill fibers.
Rib: Flat black monofilament.
Abdomen: Brown, claret, and black seal fur, mixed.
Wingcase: Dyed black turkey quill, 3 sections.
Antennae: Black goose quill fibers.

Kaufmann's Golden Stone
Hook: Extra long nymph, numbers 2-10.
Thread: Orange.
Weight: 12-20 turns lead wire, flattened.
Tail: Brown goose quill fibers.
Rib: Flat gold monofilament.
Abdomen: Orange, yellow, amber, brown seal mixed with hare's ear fur.
Wingcase. Dyed gold turkey quill, 3 sections.
Thorax: Same as abdomen.
Antennae: Brown goose quill fibers.

Gold Ribbed Hare's Ear
Hook: 1X long numbers 10-16.
Thread: Black 6/0.
Weight: 8-10 turns lead wire (optional).
Tail: Tuft of hare's poll hair.
Rib: Medium gold tinsel.
Abdomen: Tan fur from hare's mask.
Wingcase: Brown mottled turkey.
Thorax: Dark fur from hare's mask.

Pheasant Tail
Hook: 1X long numbers 10-16.

Thread: Brown 6/0.
Tail: Pheasant center tail fibers.
Rib: Gold wire.
Body: Pheasant center tail fibers, as herl.
Legs: Pheasant center tail fiber butts.

Zug Bug
Hook: 1X long numbers 10-16.
Thread: Black 6/0.
Weight: 8-10 turns lead wire (optional).
Tail: Peacock sword.
Rib: Oval silver tinsel.
Body: Peacock herl.
Hackle: Furnace, sparse.
Wingcase: Wood duck flank fibers, clipped short.

Tied-down Caddis
Hook: 1X long numbers 10-16.
Thread: Tan 6/0 (leave 6'' dangling to tie tail down).
Hackle: Ginger, palmered over body.
Body: Orange wool yarn.
Shellback: Deer body hair.
Tail: Shellback hair tied down.

WET FLIES

March Brown Spider
Hook: 1X fine dry fly numbers 10-16.
Thread: Orange 6/0.
Rib: Narrow gold tinsel.
Body: Mixed fur from hare's mask.
Hackle: Brown partridge.

Partridge and Orange
Hook: 1X fine dry fly numbers 10-16.
Thread: Orange 6/0.
Body: Orange floss.
Thorax: Hare's mask fur.
Hackle: Brown partridge.

Partridge and Green
Hook: 1X fine dry fly.
Thread: Olive 6/0.
Body: Green floss.
Thorax: Hare's mask fur.
Hackle: Gray partridge.

Appendix B - Steelhead Flies

Fall Favorite
Hook: Up eye, 2X long, 2X stout, numbers 2-8.
Thread: Black.
Body: Silver tinsel.
Hackle: Red.
Wing: Hot orange calf tail or polar bear hair.

Freight Train
Hook: Up eye, 2X long, 2X stout, numbers 2-8.
Thread: Black.
Tail: Purple hackle fibers.
Rib: Oval silver tinsel.
Body: Rear 1/4 fluorescent orange floss; 2nd 1/4 fluorescent red floss; front 1/2 black chenille.
Hackle: Purple.
Wing: White calf tail.

Green Butt Skunk
Hook: Up eye, 2X long, 2X stout, numbers 2-8.
Thread: Black.
Tail: Red saddle hackle.
Butt: Fluorescent green chenille.
Rib: Oval silver tinsel.
Body: Black chenille.
Hackle: Black.
Wing: White calf tail.

Macks Canyon
Hook: Up eye, 2x long, 2X stout, numbers 2-8.
Thread: Black.
Tail: Orange and white hackle, mixed.
Rib: Oval silver tinsel.
Body: Rear 1/3 orange wool yarn; front 2/3 black wool yarn.
Hackle: Black.
Underwing: White calf tail.
Overwing: Orange calf tail.

Purple Peril
Hook: Up eye, 2X long, 2X stout, numbers 2-8.
Thread: Black.
Tag: Oval silver tinsel.
Tail: Purple hackle.
Rib: Oval silver tinsel.
Body: Purple chenille.
Hackle: Purple.
Wing: Fox squirrel tail.

Steelhead Muddler
Hook: Up eye, 2X long, 2X stout, numbers 2-10.
Thread: Black.
Body: Flat gold tinsel.
Underwing: Gray squirrel tail.
Overwing: Mottled turkey quill.
Collar: Deer body hair.
Head: Deer hair, spun and clipped.

Above: *Wading deep, casting long, and a patient kind of faith are the keys to taking summer steelhead from the difficult water of the lower river.* LOREN IRVING

Bibliography

Aikens, C. Melvin: *Archeology of Oregon.* Portland: Bureau of Land Management, 1984.

Alt, David D. and Donald W. Hyndman: *Roadside Geology of Oregon.* Missoula, Montana: Mountain Press, 1978.

Bakeless, John, ed.: *The Journals of Lewis and Clark.* New York: New American Library, 1964.

Baldwin, Ewart M.: *Geology of Oregon.* Dubuque, Iowa: Kendall/Hunt, 1964.

Brogan, Phil F.: *East of the Cascades.* Portland: Binfords and Mort, 1964.

Brooks, Charles: *Nymph Fishing For Larger Trout.* New York: Crown, 1976.

Hafele, Rick and Dave Hughes: *Western Hatches.* Portland: Frank Amato Publications, 1981.

Hughes, Dave: *American Fly Tying Manual.* Portland: Frank Amato Publications, 1986.

Western Streamside Guide. Portland: Frank Amato Publications, 1987.

Irving, Washington: *Astoria.* Portland: Binfords and Mort, 1967.

Jackman, E. R. and R. A. Long: *The Oregon Desert.* Caldwell, Idaho: Caxton Printers, 1982.

Johnson, Daniel M., et. al.: *Atlas of Oregon Lakes.* Corvallis, Oregon: Oregon State University Press; no date (1987).

Langtry, Judge Virgil: "The Deschutes I Know". Portland: Article in *The Creel*, publication of the Flyfishers Club of Oregon, January 1980.

Luelling, Chet: "Sixty Years Ago." Portland: Article in *The Creel*, publication of the Flyfishers Club of Oregon, January, 1980.

Miskimins, R.W.: *Guide to Floating Whitewater Rivers.* Portland: Frank Amato Publications, 1987.

Nemes, Sylvester: *The Soft-Hackled Fly.* Greenwich, CT: Chatham Press, 1975.

Quinn, James M., James W. Quinn, and James G. King: *Handbook to the Deschutes River Canyon.* Sunriver, OR: Educational Adventures, 1979.

Santiam Flycasters, ed.: *Deschutes Hatch.* Salem, Oregon: Santiam Flycasters, 1983.

Snow, Berkely: *The History of the Deschutes Club.* Portland: Touchstone Press, 1966.

Above: *Fragrant mock orange blooms in late May and June, brightening the riverbanks, scenting the air, and almost defining trout fishing time along the Deschutes River.* FRANK AMATO